What God is Saying in the Book of Ephesians

GOD REVEALS HIS DEEP SECRETS TO US

Lorenzo Hill

COPYRIGHT

Copyright © by Lorenzo Hill.

All rights reserved. No part of this publication may be reproduced, distributed or transmitted in any form or by any means, including photocopying, recording, or other electronic or mechanical methods, without the prior written permission of the publisher, except in the case of brief quotations embodied in critical reviews and certain other noncommercial uses permitted by copyright law.

Scripture quotations taken from the NIV
THE HOLY BIBLE, NEW INTERNATIONAL VERSION®, NIV® Copyright © 1973, 1978, 1984, 2011 by Biblica, Inc.® Used by permission. All rights reserved worldwide.
Scripture quotations taken from the Amplified® Bible (AMP),
Copyright © 2015 by The Lockman Foundation
Used by permission. www.Lockman.org

Scripture quotations taken from the Amplified® Bible (AMPC),
Copyright © 1954, 1958, 1962, 1964, 1965, 1987 by The Lockman Foundation
Used by permission. www.Lockman.org

Scripture Taken from the HOLY BIBLE: EASY-TO-READ VERSION ©2014 by Bible League International. Used by permission.

Scripture Quotations taken from the King James Bible are from Public Domain Version

Book Layout ©2017 BookDesignTemplates.com

Cover photo from NASA free photos

What God is Saying in the Book of Ephesians/ Lorenzo Hill. — 1st ed. 2024
Copyright © 2024 by Lorenzo Hill
ISBN-13 978-0-9995992-6-6

Table of Contents

COPYRIGHT	II
PAUL'S HEAVENLY CREDENTIALS	1
SUMMARY 8	
DEVINE INSIGHTS FROM ABOVE	11
SUMMARY 16	
COMPARE THE PROPHETIC UTTERANCE IN REVELATION AND THE BOOK OF EPHESIANS	27
SUMMARY 34	
GRACE AND WHAT IT MEANS.	39
SUMMARY 48	
GOOD WORKS, HOW THEY BECOME A DRIVING FORCE IN US	55
SUMMARY 63	
THE BASIS OF OUR SIN; OUR SELFISH NATURE	73
SUMMARY 84	
PAUL EXPLAINS OUR DEFENSIVE TOOLS TO RESIST SINFUL INFLUENCES	93
SUMMARY 108	
GOD HAS TO HAVE A HOLY AND RIGHTEOUS PEOPLE TO DWELL WITH HIM	123
SUMMARY 132	
JESUS WHO HE IS AND HIS LOVE AND HIS PURPOSE	143
SUMMARY 155	
WHAT LIES BEFORE US?	159
SUMMARY 172	
POSTSCRIPT	177
APPENDIX	179
INDEX	181
SCRIPTURE REFERENCES	189
ABOUT THE AUTHOR	197

Dedicated To
Our Lord and Saviour
Jesus the Christ of Nazareth.

EPHESIANS 1:1 KING JAMES VERSION

¹ Paul, an apostle of Jesus Christ by the will of God, to the saints which are at Ephesus, and to the faithful in Christ Jesus:

EPHESIANS 4:1-15 KING JAMES VERSION

¹ I therefore, the prisoner of the Lord, beseech you that ye walk worthy of the vocation wherewith ye are called,
² With all lowliness and meekness, with longsuffering, forbearing one another in love;
³ Endeavouring to keep the unity of the Spirit in the bond of peace.
⁴ There is one body, and one Spirit, even as ye are called in one hope of your calling;
⁵ One Lord, one faith, one baptism,
⁶ One God and Father of all, who is above all, and through all, and in you all.
⁷ But unto every one of us is given grace according to the measure of the gift of Christ.
⁸ Wherefore he saith, When he ascended up on high, he led captivity captive, and gave gifts unto men.
⁹ (Now that he ascended, what is it but that he also descended first into the lower parts of the earth?
¹⁰ He that descended is the same also that ascended up far above all heavens, that he might fill all things.)
¹¹ And he gave some, apostles; and some, prophets; and some, evangelists; and some, pastors and teachers;
¹² For the perfecting of the saints, for the work of the ministry, for the edifying of the body of Christ:
¹³ Till we all come in the unity of the faith, and of the knowledge of the Son of God, unto a perfect man, unto the measure of the stature of the fulness of Christ:
¹⁴ That we henceforth be no more children, tossed to and fro, and carried about with every wind of doctrine, by the sleight of men, and cunning craftiness, whereby they lie in wait to deceive;
¹⁵ But speaking the truth in love, may grow up into him in all things, which is the head, even Christ:

1 JOHN 3:18 KING JAMES VERSION

¹⁸ My little children, let us not love in word, neither in tongue; but in deed and in truth.

1 JOHN 3:18 EASY-TO-READ VERSION

[18] My children, our love should not be only words and talk. No, our love must be real. We must show our love by the things we do.

Chapter 1

Paul's Heavenly Credentials

EPHESIANS 1:1 KING JAMES VERSION

1 Paul an apostle of Jesus Christ by the will of God, to the saints which are at Ephesus, and to the faithful in Christ Jesus:

EPHESIANS 4:1-15 KING JAMES VERSION

¹ I therefore, the prisoner of the Lord, beseech you that ye walk worthy of the vocation wherewith ye are called,
² With all lowliness and meekness, with longsuffering, forbearing one another in love;
³ Endeavouring to keep the unity of the Spirit in the bond of peace.
⁴ There is one body, and one Spirit, even as ye are called in one hope of your calling;
⁵ One Lord, one faith, one baptism,
⁶ One God and Father of all, who is above all, and through all, and in you all.
⁷ But unto every one of us is given grace according to the measure of the gift of Christ.
⁸ Wherefore he saith, When he ascended up on high, he led captivity captive, and gave gifts unto men.
⁹ (Now that he ascended, what is it but that he also descended first into the lower parts of the earth?
¹⁰ He that descended is the same also that ascended up far above all heavens, that he might fill all things.)
¹¹ And he gave some, apostles; and some, prophets; and some, evangelists; and some, pastors and teachers;
¹² For the perfecting of the saints, for the work of the ministry, for the edifying of the body of Christ:

13 Till we all come in the unity of the faith, and of the knowledge of the Son of God, unto a perfect man, unto the measure of the stature of the fulness of Christ:
14 That we henceforth be no more children, tossed to and fro, and carried about with every wind of doctrine, by the sleight of men, and cunning craftiness, whereby they lie in wait to deceive;
15 But speaking the truth in love, may grow up into him in all things, which is the head, even Christ:

Here we are told something very special Paul explains where and why he is to be seriously paid attention to. He states in a few words who he is and why he is doing this work. First, he points out that he has a special role. This role is not of his own choice or his own imagination. Unlike those who gain prominence as experts or who have gained prominence by their deeds, Paul is not one of these. He could state his previous work as a student of others and their influence in this work. No, he does not do this. He does not provide any self-will or influences from others. He is not working to build up himself as so many others do. No, he does not take any credit whatsoever for what he is sharing. Note the emphasis on sharing. Many others try to dazzle you with their achievements. No this is not about him. So, what is being said here? Again, reread this first sentence.

EPHESIANS 1:1 AMPLIFIED BIBLE

The Blessings of Redemption
1 Paul, an apostle (special messenger, personally chosen representative) of Christ Jesus (the Messiah, the Anointed), by the will of God [that is, by His purpose and choice],
To the [a]saints (God's people) [b]who are at Ephesus and are faithful and loyal and steadfast in Christ Jesus:
Footnotes
   a) *Ephesians 1:1 "Saints" refers to born-again believers. All believers are holy, that is, set apart or sanctified for God's purpose.*
   b) *Ephesians 1:1 Three early mss do not contain "at Ephesus." Some scholars suggest that this was intended as a circular letter for various churches of Asia Minor (modern Turkey), sent first to Ephesus and then to the other churches. See Paul's instruction to the Colossians in 4:16. Others believe the letter was directed only to the*

> *Ephesians because of its many personal references. The books of Ephesians, Philippians, Colossians, and Philemon are believed to have been written by Paul while he was a prisoner under house arrest in Rome (a.d. 60-62) (cf 6:20).*

He states first he is a true appointee of the Lord Jesus. Why is this so valuable? Later, we see that it is important that we know it is by the work of Jesus that his true ministers are chosen and appointed. Yes, this is an honor bestowed by Jesus Himself. Not something someone has attained by human effort or deed. It is not something that someone feels he should be or do but it is indeed something which has been structured by Jesus and He and He only should be given credit for this information or revelation. Review the intro John provides in the presentation of the book of Revelations. Reread this quote.

> **REVELATION 1:1-3 NEW INTERNATIONAL VERSION**
>
> *Prologue*
> *¹ The revelation from Jesus Christ, which God gave him to show his servants what must soon take place. He made it known by sending his angel to his servant John,*
> *² who testifies to everything he saw—that is, the word of God and the testimony of Jesus Christ.*
> *³ Blessed is the one who reads aloud the words of this prophecy, and blessed are those who hear it and take to heart what is written in it, because the time is near.*

Here again we see the emphasis for this is placed on the Lord Jesus not on John or who he is or what he has done or any earthly credentials. We see the emphasis is on the Son of God, not man nor the works of men but the authority for this is from above.

The Lord wants us to see in both works not the arm of flesh but the arm of the divine. Man likes to toot his own horn and show how gifted he is and what the world sees as authoritative. No this is not that at all. We have here a glimpse into the work of the divine explicitly for us to see the love of the divine and His work in the lives of men.

So not only are we provided the commission from Jesus, but we are told that the Father is also involved and it is a joint appointment determined by them alone. It is not for Paul's self-esteem that this work is presented but for us to understand more about the two most important beings which ever will be. Yes, folks open your eyes and stop looking to men but look into the heavens and what they behold. Open your understanding, for what we are being shown is more than mere words or a story to be repeated but this is divine and we are to get a further glimpse into their character and relationship between us and them.

So now we can get to know more about the workings of God from the source not something that man has tried to understand on his own, but what the real truth is. Yes, this is a genuine revelation of the Lord and we need to pay particular attention to this. It is the basis of all Paul is called to do and the reasons behind what he has been led to be and do. Just as the apostle John, Paul is called to represent to us the divine and not the learning of man gained through his limited observation. This is the truth in its purest form. This is unadulterated material. Provided to lead us into all truth stated to provide us a more perfect view of the work of the Lord and the works of darkness. Again, from scripture hear the word of the Lord.

DEUTERONOMY 29:3-5 NEW INTERNATIONAL VERSION

3 With your own eyes you saw those great trials, those signs and great wonders.
4 But to this day the Lord has not given you a mind that understands or eyes that see or ears that hear.
5 Yet the Lord says, "During the forty years that I led you through the wilderness, your clothes did not wear out, nor did the sandals on your feet.

JEREMIAH 6:9-11 KING JAMES VERSION

9 Thus saith the Lord of hosts, They shall throughly glean the remnant of Israel as a vine: turn back thine hand as a grapegatherer into the baskets.
10 To whom shall I speak, and give warning, that they may hear? behold, their ear is uncircumcised, and they cannot hearken: behold, the word of the Lord is unto them a reproach; they have no delight in it.
11 Therefore I am full of the fury of the Lord; I am weary with holding in: I will pour it out upon the children abroad, and upon the assembly of young men together: for even the husband with the wife shall be taken, the aged with him that is full of days.

EZEKIEL 12:1-3 NEW INTERNATIONAL VERSION

The Exile Symbolized
¹ The word of the Lord came to me:
² "Son of man, you are living among a rebellious people. They have eyes to see but do not see and ears to hear but do not hear, for they are a rebellious people.
³ "Therefore, son of man, pack your belongings for exile and in the daytime, as they watch, set out and go from where you are to another place. Perhaps they will understand, though they are a rebellious people.

MARK 4:22-24 NEW INTERNATIONAL VERSION

²² For whatever is hidden is meant to be disclosed, and whatever is concealed is meant to be brought out into the open. ²³ If anyone has ears to hear, let them hear."
²⁴ "Consider carefully what you hear," he continued. "With the measure you use, it will be measured to you—and even more.

MARK 4:1-10 NEW INTERNATIONAL VERSION

The Parable of the Sower
¹ Again Jesus began to teach by the lake. The crowd that gathered around him was so large that he got into a boat and sat in it out on the lake, while all the people were along the shore at the water's edge.
² He taught them many things by parables, and in his teaching said: ³ "Listen! A farmer went out to sow his seed.
⁴ As he was scattering the seed, some fell along the path, and the birds came and ate it up.
⁵ Some fell on rocky places, where it did not have much soil. It sprang up quickly, because the soil was shallow.
⁶ But when the sun came up, the plants were scorched, and they withered because they had no root.
⁷ Other seed fell among thorns, which grew up and choked the plants, so that they did not bear grain.
⁸ Still other seed fell on good soil. It came up, grew and produced a crop, some multiplying thirty, some sixty, some a hundred times."
⁹ Then Jesus said, "Whoever has ears to hear, let them hear."
¹⁰ When he was alone, the Twelve and the others around him asked him about the parables.

MARK 8:17-19 NEW INTERNATIONAL VERSION

17 Aware of their discussion, Jesus asked them: "Why are you talking about having no bread? Do you still not see or understand? Are your hearts hardened?
18 Do you have eyes but fail to see, and ears but fail to hear? And don't you remember?
19 When I broke the five loaves for the five thousand, how many basketfuls of pieces did you pick up?"
"Twelve," they replied.

2 TIMOTHY 4:2-4 KING JAMES VERSION

2 Preach the word; be instant in season, out of season; reprove, rebuke, exhort with all long suffering and doctrine.

3 For the time will come when they will not endure sound doctrine; but after their own lusts shall they heap to themselves teachers, having itching ears;
4 And they shall turn away their ears from the truth, and shall be turned unto fables.

REVELATION 2:10-12 NEW INTERNATIONAL VERSION

10 Do not be afraid of what you are about to suffer. I tell you, the devil will put some of you in prison to test you, and you will suffer persecution for ten days. Be faithful, even to the point of death, and I will give you life as your victor's crown.
11 Whoever has ears, let them hear what the Spirit says to the churches. The one who is victorious will not be hurt at all by the second death.

Now we should be able to understand how important the fact of God's will being spread by the fact that Paul was a person chosen by God and as such he brings insights which are the will of God. The action of one being chosen by God to represent His will is shed throughout scripture. We are even told that prophetic utterance is only received by the will of God. Our very existence is based on His will.

2 PETER 1:20-21 EASY-TO-READ VERSION

20 Most important of all, you must understand this: No prophecy in the Scriptures comes from the prophet's own understanding.

21 No prophecy ever came from what some person wanted to say. But people were led by the Holy Spirit and spoke words from God.

1 SAMUEL 2:26-35 EASY-TO-READ VERSION

26 The boy Samuel kept growing. He was pleasing to the Lord and to the people.

The Terrible Prophecy About Eli's Family

27 A man of God came to Eli and said, "The Lord says, 'I appeared to your ancestors[a] when they were slaves of Pharaoh.

28 From all the tribes of Israel, I chose your tribe to be my priests. I chose them to offer sacrifices on my altar, to burn incense, and wear the ephod. I also let your tribe have the meat from the sacrifices that the Israelites give to me.

29 So why don't you respect these gifts and sacrifices? You honor your sons more than me. You become fat eating the best parts of the meat that the Israelites bring to me.'

30 "The Lord, the God of Israel, promised that your father's family would serve him forever. But now the Lord says, 'That will never be! I will honor people who honor me, but bad things will happen to those who refuse to respect me.

31 The time is coming when I will destroy all your descendants. No one in your family will live to be an old man.

32 Good things will happen to Israel, but you will see bad things happening at home.[b] No one in your family will live to be an old man.

33 There is only one man I will save to serve as priest at my altar. He will live until his eyes wear out and his strength is gone. But all of your descendants will die by the sword.[c]

34 I will give you a sign to show that these things will come true. Your two sons, Hophni and Phinehas, will die on the same day.

35 I will choose a priest I can trust. This priest will listen to me and do what I want. I will make his family strong, and he will always serve before my chosen king.[d]

Footnotes
a) 1 Samuel 2:27 ancestors Literally, "father's house." See "ancestor" in the Word List.
b) 1 Samuel 2:32 but you … at home These words are not in the ancient Greek version or the Hebrew scrolls from Qumran.
c) 1 Samuel 2:33 by the sword This is found in the ancient Greek version and a Hebrew scroll from Qumran. The standard Hebrew text has "like men."

    d) 1 Samuel 2:35 chosen king Literally, "anointed one."

    Now there is one more thing to point out in this beginning salutation. Paul is directing this message to not only those at Ephesus but to all those who are faithful. Yes, the fact that we need to understand that the importance of what is contained in this letter Paul is writing. It is for all whom God has chosen and who faithfully serve Him. You can see from this God is willing to expose Himself to those who are faithful not just a few in Ephesus but to all for all time. There is no limitation on what is being shared as we can see. Yes, this is a timeless message not limited to a particular situation, place, or people. These words Paul is delivering are eternal and without limitation. It applies just as much to us today as it did the day Paul was directed to share this message. So, we need to understand the value of what is being shared. You see Paul is sharing what he has been directed to share by the will of God through the power of Jesus and the Holy spirit just as John was in the book of Revelation.

Summary

    So, Let Us allow the Spirit and our Lord Jesus to bring us to understand the things which He is presenting here in this prophetic utterance. In this there is not a complete picture, but an overview of things man needs to understand. Just as we are only provided an overview in the creation narrative, not a detailed description, we are given a snapshot of the love of God the Father for us all. He gives us enough to know who He is and what are the driving forces which man has in this life.

    That is why it is so important for us to accept that Paul is a servant of the Most High and it is by the choice of the Most High God Paul has been provided the duty to deliver this message to us. Here we see the will of the Lord in action. We should see here this is an honor no man takes on himself. It is one only God can provide. Can't we see it? He is creating a new thing. This is His established pattern until we come to the same point which Enoch arrived at and where Jesus was and is and always will be. So, until we are at that point God appoints certain men and women for this purpose. That is to lead us to perfection.

Pay strict attention to what Paul is being led to share with us because it contains things which God wants us to clearly understand.

In the second verse we are told that this is a letter from both God the Father and Jesus not Paul.

EPHESIANS 1:2 KING JAMES VERSION

² Grace be to you, and peace, from God our Father, and from the Lord Jesus Christ.

It should be plain from this that the Lord and the Father God have agreed on what we need to hear from them at this time. This is them dictating to Paul the words in this text.

CHAPTER 2

Devine Insights From Above

EPHESIANS 1:3 KING JAMES VERSION

³ Blessed be the God and Father of our Lord Jesus Christ, who hath blessed us with all spiritual blessings in heavenly places in Christ:

The Lord uses Paul to address us from Him and Jesus providing information which we should know but many do not understand. First is the fact that he has provided us with all spiritual blessings but they are not here on earth. They reside in heaven not here on earth. We are told Jesus has the authority and is responsible for these. Here we see God has not withheld any of these, yet they are placed in trustworthy hands. You see Jesus has proven Himself to be trusted and is wise and enough to accept this responsibility. All these are at His disposal to disseminate as needed to whomever and however He wishes. There are no limitations which we are told that have been placed on Jesus in regard to the use of these spiritual gifts. Yet we can figure this out from the fact the Father has not just provided them to us randomly. There must be a deliberate and wise use of these. These must be immensely powerful, and we cannot yet be trusted with them. So, we are told they exist and only Jesus has the keys to unlock these.

Now we continue to hear more about the wisdom and plans of the almighty. Look at the next few verses.

EPHESIANS 1:4-6 KING JAMES VERSION

⁴ According as he hath chosen us in him before the foundation of the world, that we should be holy and without blame before him in love:

⁵ Having predestinated us unto the adoption of children by Jesus Christ to himself, according to the good pleasure of his will,
⁶ To the praise of the glory of his grace, wherein he hath made us accepted in the beloved.

EPHESIANS 1:4-6 EASY-TO-READ VERSION

⁴ In Christ, he chose us before the world was made. He chose us in love to be his holy people—people who could stand before him without any fault.
⁵ And before the world was made, God decided to make us his own children through Jesus Christ. This was what God wanted, and it pleased him to do it.
⁶ And this brings praise to God because of his wonderful grace. God gave that grace to us freely. He gave us that grace in Christ, the one he loves.

Here we are told that even before the creation of the world God provided a way to save us from ourselves (that selfish nature). Yes, He wants us to choose the necessary conditions which are required for us to exist in His presence. He has set up a plan to guarantee that we can be Holy and without blame before Him. The path to this has been predetermined to be through the work of Jesus and the work He is performing to reshape us into this perfect state. God knew before we ever existed that there needed to be a path for this to happen because we would not be able to do it on our own. He wanted to be sure that there would not be any mistakes or problems with this process. So, He produced the perfect plan of salvation. He knew that only He with Jesus could guarantee the success of this plan. The Lord made us and knew that because we have freedom to choose it would take something outside of us to transform us so that we can be Holy and without blame. He did not make us a bunch of robots or clones of Himself. He made us as individuals with freedom to choose right and wrong and allowed forces to exist so that we would have the freedom to choose to either accept this option or turn it down. Notice He willed before we were created that we should have a pathway to escape our human nature and be endowed with a divine nature. Because of His unfailing love we have the choice to accept this predetermined or predestined path to Him. The Lord established (predestined) this plan because of His pure love for us and His understanding of human desires and our inability to overcome them. We all were provided with some problem areas in us and only He can correct these.

ECCLESIASTES 7:20 AMPLIFIED BIBLE

[20] *Indeed, there is not a righteous man on earth who always does good and who never sins.*

ROMANS 3:23-24 EASY-TO-READ VERSION

[23] *All have sinned and are not good enough to share God's divine greatness.*
[24] *They are made right with God by his grace. This is a free gift. They are made right with God by being made free from sin through Jesus Christ.*

Oh, we are also told there are some here who have already had the law implanted in their heart and they are a law unto themselves. If you are one of these how fortunate you are. You don't have that struggle we face with good and evil but there still is the requirement for those who have the law implanted within to accept Jesus as their savior.

Romans 2:11-15 Amplified Bible

[11] *For God shows no partiality [no arbitrary favoritism; with Him one person is not more important than another].*
[12] *For all who have sinned without the Law will also perish without [regard to] the Law, and all who have sinned under the Law will be judged and condemned by the Law.*
[13] *For it is not those who merely hear the Law [as it is read aloud] who are just or righteous before God, but it is those who [actually] obey the Law who will be [a]justified [pronounced free of the guilt of sin and declared acceptable to Him].*
[14] *When Gentiles, who do not have the Law [since it was given only to Jews], do [b]instinctively the things the Law requires [guided only by their conscience], they are a law to themselves, though they do not have the Law.*
[15] *They show that the [c]essential requirements of the Law are written in their hearts; and their conscience [their sense of right and wrong, their moral choices] bearing witness and their thoughts alternately accusing or perhaps defending them*
   Footnotes
   a. *Romans 2:13 Because of one's personal faith in Jesus Christ as Savior, God graciously credits His righteousness*

> to the believer. Justification denotes a legal standing with God as designated only by God. God declares a believer to be acquitted or innocent, then designates the believer to be brought into right standing before Him.
> b. Romans 2:14 Lit by nature.
> c. Romans 2:15 Lit work of the Law.
>
> ### ROMANS 2:11-15 EASY-TO-READ VERSION
>
> [11] *God judges everyone the same. It doesn't matter who they are.*
> [12] *People who have the law and those who have never heard of the law are all the same when they sin. People who don't have the law and are sinners will be lost. And, in the same way, those who have the law and are sinners will be judged by the law.*
> [13] *Hearing the law does not make people right with God. They will be right before him only if they always do what the law says.*
> [14] *Those who are not Jews don't have the law. But when they naturally do what the law commands without even knowing the law, then they are their own law. This is true even though they don't have the written law.*
> [15] *They show that in their hearts they know what is right and wrong, the same as the law commands, and their consciences agree. Sometimes their thoughts tell them that they have done wrong, and this makes them guilty. And sometimes their thoughts tell them that they have done right, and this makes them not guilty.*

Grace is now defined for us. The work of Jesus was preordained to provide us with the needed path to Holiness and righteousness necessary for us to live with Him. It is stated in terms of a person who is an orphan. So, He terms this an adoption. So, it is a choice made by Him so that we could find our way to His presence. We must come to understand that grace is initiated by God not us. He is in full control of this process. So, our only option is to accept or reject this offer. He takes responsibility for the relationship and ours is to accept or reject.

Does this mean that man was created with the inability to achieve this state of divinity on his own. Yes, it does. You see God placed within us the ability to know right from wrong. Yes, each one is endowed from birth with a conscience. Yet this alone cannot save him. This is because we all have the ability to override the sense of right and wrong due to our innate ability to choose not to follow this inbuilt mechanism to stay on the narrow path of righteous behavior. It is our sense of "me first" which comes into play and this causes us to go off course from the desired end of being Holy and righteous so that we need help to attain to the state which God requires for us to meet the final state we need to be in to reside with Him forever.

ROMANS 2:14-16 EASY-TO-READ VERSION

14 Those who are not Jews don't have the law. But when they naturally do what the law commands without even knowing the law, then they are their own law. This is true even though they don't have the written law.
15 They show that in their hearts they know what is right and wrong, the same as the law commands, and their consciences agree. Sometimes their thoughts tell them that they have done wrong, and this makes them guilty. And sometimes their thoughts tell them that they have done right, and this makes them not guilty.
16 All this will happen on the day when God will judge people's secret thoughts through Jesus Christ. This is part of the Good News that I tell everyone.

1 TIMOTHY 4:1-3 EASY-TO-READ VERSION

A Warning About False Teachers
1 The Spirit clearly says that in the last times some will turn away from what we believe. They will obey spirits that tell lies. And they will follow the teachings of demons.
2 Those teachings come through people who tell lies and trick others. These evil people cannot see what is right and what is wrong. It is like their conscience has been destroyed with a hot iron. 3 They say that it is wrong to marry. And they say that there are some foods that people must not eat. But God made these foods, and those who believe and who understand the truth can eat them with thanks.

TITUS 1:14-16 EASY-TO-READ VERSION

14 and they will stop paying attention to the stories told by those Jews. They will stop following the commands of those who have turned away from the truth.
15 To people who are pure, everything is pure. But to those who are full of sin and don't believe, nothing is pure. Really, their thinking has become evil and their consciences have been ruined.

[16] They say they know God, but the evil things they do show that they don't accept him. They are disgusting. They refuse to obey God and are not capable of doing anything good.

1 PETER 3:20-22 EASY-TO-READ VERSION

[20] Those were the spirits who refused to obey God long ago in the time of Noah. God was waiting patiently for people while Noah was building the big boat. And only a few—eight in all—were saved in the boat through the floodwater.
[21] And that water is like baptism, which now saves you. Baptism is not the washing of dirt from the body. It is asking God for a clean conscience. It saves you because Jesus Christ was raised from death.
[22] Now he has gone into heaven. He is at God's right side and rules over angels, authorities, and powers.

Summary

We can see from this no one is predestined to fail or succeed. It is that we cannot achieve the state of perfection on our own. Only Jesus has done this and only He can be the course correction we need in life. He has the whole arsenal of tools needed to accomplish this as He has control of all Spiritual blessings.

Yes the choice we make whenever the Holy Spirit entices us to accept the help He provides so that we are able to be made perfect in conduct and thought to be able to dwell in God's presence. The plan of redemption was put in place long before we were created because of the eternal Love which God and Jesus have and which they can provide to us through the work of the Holy Spirit.

JOHN 8:8-10 KING JAMES VERSION

[8] And again he stooped down, and wrote on the ground.
[9] And they which heard it, being convicted by their own conscience, went out one by one, beginning at the eldest, even unto the last: and Jesus was left alone, and the woman standing in the midst.

¹⁰ When Jesus had lifted up himself, and saw none but the woman, he said unto her, Woman, where are those thine accusers? hath no man condemned thee?

ACTS 24:15-17 KING JAMES VERSION

¹⁵ And have hope toward God, which they themselves also allow, that there shall be a resurrection of the dead, both of the just and unjust.
¹⁶ And herein do I exercise myself, to have always a conscience void to offence toward God, and toward men.
¹⁷ Now after many years I came to bring alms to my nation, and offerings.

ROMANS 2:14-16 KING JAMES VERSION

¹⁴ For when the Gentiles, which have not the law, do by nature the things contained in the law, these, having not the law, are a law unto themselves:
¹⁵ Which shew the work of the law written in their hearts, their conscience also bearing witness, and their thoughts the mean while accusing or else excusing one another;)
¹⁶ In the day when God shall judge the secrets of men by Jesus Christ according to my gospel.

ROMANS 2:14-16 EASY-TO-READ VERSION

¹⁴ Those who are not Jews don't have the law. But when they naturally do what the law commands without even knowing the law, then they are their own law. This is true even though they don't have the written law.
¹⁵ They show that in their hearts they know what is right and wrong, the same as the law commands, and their consciences agree. Sometimes their thoughts tell them that they have done wrong, and this makes them guilty. And sometimes their thoughts tell them that they have done right, and this makes them not guilty.
¹⁶ All this will happen on the day when God will judge people's secret thoughts through Jesus Christ. This is part of the Good News that I tell everyone.

ROMANS 9:1-3 KING JAMES VERSION

¹ I say the truth in Christ, I lie not, my conscience also bearing me witness in the Holy Ghost,
² That I have great heaviness and continual sorrow in my heart.

³ For I could wish that myself were accursed from Christ for my brethren, my kinsmen according to the flesh:

ROMANS 9:1-3 EASY-TO-READ VERSION

God and the Jewish People
¹ I am in Christ and I am telling you the truth. I am not lying. And my conscience, ruled by the Holy Spirit, agrees that what I say now is true.
² I have great sorrow and always feel much sadness
³ for my own people. They are my brothers and sisters, my earthly family. I wish I could help them. I would even have a curse on me and cut myself off from Christ if that would help them.

1 CORINTHIANS 8:11-13 KING JAMES VERSION

¹¹ And through thy knowledge shall the weak brother perish, for whom Christ died?
¹² But when ye sin so against the brethren, and wound their weak conscience, ye sin against Christ.
¹³ Wherefore, if meat make my brother to offend, I will eat no flesh while the world standeth, lest I make my brother to offend.

1 CORINTHIANS 8:11-13 EASY-TO-READ VERSION

¹¹ So this weak brother or sister—someone Christ died for—is lost because of your better understanding.
¹² When you sin against your brothers and sisters in Christ in this way and you hurt them by causing them to do things they feel are wrong, you are also sinning against Christ.
¹³ So if the food I eat makes another believer fall into sin, I will never eat meat again. I will stop eating meat, so that I will not make my brother or sister sin.

2 CORINTHIANS 1:11-13 AMPLIFIED BIBLE

¹¹ while you join in helping us by your prayers. Then thanks will be given by many persons on our behalf for the gracious gift [of deliverance] granted to us through the prayers of many [believers].
Paul's Integrity
¹² This is our [reason for] proud confidence: our conscience testifies that we have conducted ourselves in the world [in general], and especially toward you, with pure motives and godly sincerity, not in human wisdom, but in the grace of God [that is, His gracious lovingkindness that leads people to Christ and

spiritual maturity]. *¹³ For we write you nothing other than what you read and understand [there is no double meaning in what we say]. And I hope you will [accurately] understand [divine things] until the end;*

Here we can find scripture which leads us to understand when the Spirit is allowed to do so by us.

HEBREWS 9:13-15 KING JAMES VERSION

¹³ For if the blood of bulls and of goats, and the ashes of an heifer sprinkling the unclean, sanctifieth to the purifying of the flesh:
¹⁴ How much more shall the blood of Christ, who through the eternal Spirit offered himself without spot to God, purge your conscience from dead works to serve the living God?
¹⁵ And for this cause he is the mediator of the new testament, that by means of death, for the redemption of the transgressions that were under the first testament, they which are called might receive the promise of eternal inheritance.

1 PETER 3:20-22 KING JAMES VERSION

²⁰ Which sometime were disobedient, when once the longsuffering of God waited in the days of Noah, while the ark was a preparing, wherein few, that is, eight souls were saved by water.
²¹ The like figure whereunto even baptism doth also now save us (not the putting away of the filth of the flesh, but the answer of a good conscience toward God,) by the resurrection of Jesus Christ:
²² Who is gone into heaven, and is on the right hand of God; angels and authorities and powers being made subject unto him.

1 PETER 3:20-22 EASY-TO-READ VERSION

²⁰ Those were the spirits who refused to obey God long ago in the time of Noah. God was waiting patiently for people while Noah was building the big boat. And only a few—eight in all—were saved in the boat through the floodwater.
²¹ And that water is like baptism, which now saves you. Baptism is not the washing of dirt from the body. It is asking God for a clean conscience. It saves you because Jesus Christ was raised from death.
²² Now he has gone into heaven. He is at God's right side and rules over angels, authorities, and powers.

ROMANS 2:14-16 AMPLIFIED BIBLE

14 When Gentiles, who do not have the Law [since it was given only to Jews], do [a]instinctively the things the Law requires [guided only by their conscience], they are a law to themselves, though they do not have the Law.

15 They show that the [b]essential requirements of the Law are written in their hearts; and their conscience [their sense of right and wrong, their moral choices] bearing witness and their thoughts alternately accusing or perhaps defending them

16 on that day when, [c]as my gospel proclaims, God will judge the secrets [all the hidden thoughts and concealed sins] of men through Christ Jesus.

Footnotes
- a) Romans 2:14 Lit by nature.
- b) Romans 2:15 Lit work of the Law.
- c) Romans 2:16 Lit according to my gospel.

Finally, I am led to emphasize the importance of us being one in our beliefs. We are to be like minded in the things which Jesus tells us about Him and God. We need to understand that what we pass on to others and what we live out should not be any different from what Jesus did when He was present on earth. I was so excited the other day when one of our fellow evangelists and I were discussing what the truth is based on what we have been told in scripture. As we discussed the work of the Holy Spirit and the commandments of Jesus and the teachings, they have provided us in scripture and His insights into what they truly mean not how we interpret them, we were in total agreement with these things. Now we did not agree on the way each of us were called to bring about the kingdom or our individual roles we each had the same beliefs of the gospel and its implementation according to the guidance we have been provided. Does this mean we are clones of each other? No, it does not mean he is still himself and I am still me, but we are one in the spirit and one in the Lord. We are being incorporated into the kingdom. The emphasis Paul and the other apostles and prophets provided us becoming one is something which we cannot bypass, ignore, or put aside. It is imperative that this occurs. Look at this again in several places in scripture.

1 SAMUEL 2:34-36 KING JAMES VERSION

[34] And this shall be a sign unto thee, that shall come upon thy two sons, on Hophni and Phinehas; in one day they shall die both of them.
[35] And I will raise me up a faithful priest, that shall do according to that which is in mine heart and in my mind: and I will build him a sure house; and he shall walk before mine anointed for ever.
[36] And it shall come to pass, that every one that is left in thine house shall come and crouch to him for a piece of silver and a morsel of bread, and shall say, Put me, I pray thee, into one of the priests' offices, that I may eat a piece of bread.

EXODUS 35:20-22 KING JAMES VERSION

[20] And all the congregation of the children of Israel departed from the presence of Moses.
[21] And they came, every one whose heart stirred him up, and every one whom his spirit made willing, and they brought the Lord's offering to the work of the tabernacle of the congregation, and for all his service, and for the holy garments.
[22] And they came, both men and women, as many as were willing hearted, and brought bracelets, and earrings, and rings, and tablets, all jewels of gold: and every man that offered offered an offering of gold unto the Lord.

JEREMIAH 32:37-40 KING JAMES VERSION

[37] Behold, I will gather them out of all countries, whither I have driven them in mine anger, and in my fury, and in great wrath; and I will bring them again unto this place, and I will cause them to dwell safely:
[38] And they shall be my people, and I will be their God:
[39] And I will give them one heart, and one way, that they may fear me for ever, for the good of them, and of their children after them:
[40] And I will make an everlasting covenant with them, that I will not turn away from them, to do them good; but I will put my fear in their hearts, that they shall not depart from me.

EZEKIEL 11:15-20 KING JAMES VERSION

[15] Son of man, thy brethren, even thy brethren, the men of thy kindred, and all the house of Israel wholly, are they unto whom

the inhabitants of Jerusalem have said, Get you far from the Lord: unto us is this land given in possession.

[16] Therefore say, Thus saith the Lord God; Although I have cast them far off among the heathen, and although I have scattered them among the countries, yet will I be to them as a little sanctuary in the countries where they shall come.

[17] Therefore say, Thus saith the Lord God; I will even gather you from the people, and assemble you out of the countries where ye have been scattered, and I will give you the land of Israel.

[18] And they shall come thither, and they shall take away all the detestable things thereof and all the abominations thereof from thence.

[19] And I will give them one heart, and I will put a new spirit within you; and I will take the stony heart out of their flesh, and will give them an heart of flesh:

[20] That they may walk in my statutes, and keep mine ordinances, and do them: and they shall be my people, and I will be their God.

MATTHEW 13:18-25 EASY-TO-READ VERSION

Jesus Explains the Story About Seed

[18] "So listen to the meaning of that story about the farmer:

[19] "What about the seed that fell by the path? That is like the people who hear the teaching about God's kingdom but do not understand it. The Evil One comes and takes away what was planted in their hearts.

[20] "And what about the seed that fell on rocky ground? That is like the people who hear the teaching and quickly and gladly accept it. [21] But they do not let the teaching go deep into their lives. They keep it only a short time. As soon as trouble or persecution comes because of the teaching they accepted, they give up.

[22] "And what about the seed that fell among the thorny weeds? That is like the people who hear the teaching but let worries about this life and love for money stop it from growing. So it does not produce a crop in their lives.

[23] "But what about the seed that fell on the good ground? That is like the people who hear the teaching and understand it. They grow and produce a good crop, sometimes 100 times more, sometimes 60 times more, and sometimes 30 times more."

A Story About Wheat and Weeds

[24] Then Jesus used another story to teach them. Jesus said, "God's kingdom is like a man who planted good seed in his field. 25 That

night, while everyone was asleep, the man's enemy came and planted weeds among the wheat and then left.

ACTS 2:45-47 KING JAMES VERSION

45 And sold their possessions and goods, and parted them to all men, as every man had need.
46 And they, continuing daily with one accord in the temple, and breaking bread from house to house, did eat their meat with gladness and singleness of heart,
47 Praising God, and having favour with all the people. And the Lord added to the church daily such as should be saved.

ACTS 4:31-33 KING JAMES VERSION

31 And when they had prayed, the place was shaken where they were assembled together; and they were all filled with the Holy Ghost, and they spake the word of God with boldness.
32 And the multitude of them that believed were of one heart and of one soul: neither said any of them that ought of the things which he possessed was his own; but they had all things common.
33 And with great power gave the apostles witness of the resurrection of the Lord Jesus: and great grace was upon them all.

ROMANS 2:14-16 KING JAMES VERSION

14 For when the Gentiles, which have not the law, do by nature the things contained in the law, these, having not the law, are a law unto themselves:
15 Which shew the work of the law written in their hearts, their conscience also bearing witness, and their thoughts the mean while accusing or else excusing one another;)
16 In the day when God shall judge the secrets of men by Jesus Christ according to my gospel.

1 CORINTHIANS 6:16-18 EASY-TO-READ VERSION

16 The Scriptures say, "The two people will become one."[a] So you should know that anyone who is joined with a prostitute becomes one with her in body.
17 But anyone who is joined with the Lord is one with him in spirit.
18 So run away from sexual sin. It involves the body in a way that no other sin does. So if you commit sexual sin, you are sinning against your own body.
   Footnotes
   a) 1 Corinthians 6:16 Quote from Gen. 2:24.

GENESIS 5:24 EASY-TO-READ VERSION

²⁴ One day Enoch was walking with God, and he disappeared. God took him.[a]

Footnotes
a) Genesis 5:24 Or "Enoch pleased God. Enoch disappeared. God took him."

EPHESIANS 4:1-15 KING JAMES VERSION

¹ *I therefore, the prisoner of the Lord, beseech you that ye walk worthy of the vocation wherewith ye are called,*
² *With all lowliness and meekness, with longsuffering, forbearing one another in love;*
³ *Endeavouring to keep the unity of the Spirit in the bond of peace.*
⁴ *There is one body, and one Spirit, even as ye are called in one hope of your calling;*
⁵ *One Lord, one faith, one baptism,*
⁶ *One God and Father of all, who is above all, and through all, and in you all.*
⁷ *But unto every one of us is given grace according to the measure of the gift of Christ.*
⁸ *Wherefore he saith, When he ascended up on high, he led captivity captive, and gave gifts unto men.*
⁹ *(Now that he ascended, what is it but that he also descended first into the lower parts of the earth?*
¹⁰ *He that descended is the same also that ascended up far above all heavens, that he might fill all things.)*
¹¹ *And he gave some, apostles; and some, prophets; and some, evangelists; and some, pastors and teachers;*
¹² *For the perfecting of the saints, for the work of the ministry, for the edifying of the body of Christ:*
¹³ *Till we all come in the unity of the faith, and of the knowledge of the Son of God, unto a perfect man, unto the measure of the stature of the fulness of Christ:*
¹⁴ *That we henceforth be no more children, tossed to and fro, and carried about with every wind of doctrine, by the sleight of men, and cunning craftiness, whereby they lie in wait to deceive;*
¹⁵ *But speaking the truth in love, may grow up into him in all things, which is the head, even Christ:*

PHILIPPIANS 2:1-3 EASY-TO-READ VERSION

Be United and Care for Each Other

¹ Think about what we have in Christ: the encouragement he has brought us, the comfort of his love, our sharing in his Spirit, and the mercy and kindness he has shown us. If you enjoy these blessings,
² then do what will make my joy complete: Agree with each other, and show your love for each other. Be united in your goals and in the way you think.
³ In whatever you do, don't let selfishness or pride be your guide. Be humble, and honor others more than yourselves.

ROMANS 15:4-6 KING JAMES VERSION

⁴ For whatsoever things were written aforetime were written for our learning, that we through patience and comfort of the scriptures might have hope.
⁵ Now the God of patience and consolation grant you to be likeminded one toward another according to Christ Jesus:
⁶ That ye may with one mind and one mouth glorify God, even the Father of our Lord Jesus Christ.

ROMANS 15:4-12 AMPLIFIED BIBLE

⁴ For whatever was written in earlier times was written for our instruction, so that through endurance and the encouragement of the Scriptures we might have hope and overflow with confidence in His promises.
⁵ Now may the God who gives endurance and who supplies encouragement grant that you be of the same mind with one another according to Christ Jesus,
⁶ so that with one accord you may with one voice glorify and praise and honor the God and Father of our Lord Jesus Christ.
⁷ Therefore, [continue to] accept and welcome one another, just as Christ has accepted and welcomed us to the glory of [our great] God.
⁸ For I tell you that Christ has become a servant and a minister to the circumcision (Jews) on behalf of God's truth, to confirm and verify the promises made to the fathers,
⁹ and for the Gentiles to glorify God for His mercy [to them, since God had no covenant with them]. As it is written and forever remains written,
"Therefore I praise You among the Gentiles,
And sing praises to Your name."
¹⁰ Again it says,
"Rejoice and celebrate, O Gentiles, along with His people."

> **¹¹ And again,**
> *"Praise the Lord all you Gentiles,*
> *And let all the peoples praise Him!"*
> **¹² Again Isaiah says,**
> *"There shall be a root of [a]Jesse,*
> *He who arises to rule [as King] over the Gentiles,*
> *In Him shall the Gentiles hope."*
>
> **Footnotes**
> a) Romans 15:12 Jesse was the father of David the king, and Jesus (the Messiah) was a descendant of David.

In the scriptures above we find quotes from scripture in Romans chapter 15 which come from previous written scripture which we do not find in our cannon of scripture. These are proof that there have been many plain and precious things which have been removed from scripture. These are some of those. As we should see, someone has been altering scripture in ways that we have not seen and part of this has to do with the books which are referred to which we do not have now. When these are allowed to be found our understanding of God and His ways will be amplified to the nth degree., infinitely. Until then we must search the entire scripture to gain wisdom and knowledge.

CHAPTER 3

Compare the Prophetic Utterance in Revelation and the Book of Ephesians

This is primarily a repeat of the chapter provided in the book Revelation Part 1. You see even when we are provided the word of the Lord we can easily be swayed by the things of everyday life and our dealing with our fleshly desires, so I am led to add this interlude at this point to show even when God's power is evident, we easily get distracted and we focus on the wrong things. Yes, like us we let the mundane override the divine and are influenced by more easily by today than life everlasting.

> **REVELATION 2:1-7 KING JAMES VERSION (KJV)**
> *¹ Unto the angel of the Church of Ephesus write; These things saith he that holdeth the seven stars in his right hand, who walketh in the midst of the seven golden candlesticks;*
> *² I know thy works, and thy labour, and thy patience, and how thou canst not bear them which are evil: and thou hast tried them which say they are apostles, and are not, and hast found them liars:*
> *³ And hast borne, and hast patience, and for my name's sake hast laboured, and hast not fainted.*
> *⁴ Nevertheless I have somewhat against thee, because thou hast left thy first love.*

⁵ Remember therefore from whence thou art fallen, and repent, and do the first works; or else I will come unto thee quickly, and will remove thy candlestick out of his place, except thou repent.
⁶ But this thou hast, that thou hatest the deeds of the Nicolaitanes, which I also hate.
⁷ He that hath an ear, let him hear what the Spirit saith unto the Churches; To him that overcometh will I give to eat of the tree of life, which is in the midst of the paradise of God.

Again, it took the work of the Holy Spirit to get me to know this is the same group of believers that was being addressed in the letter to the Ephesians. Here, Jesus is stating through prophetic utterance what he sees in the Church at Ephesus (or the Ephesians as they are called in Paul's letter). We can compare the letter which Paul wrote years earlier and how this group's attitudes are now different. Jesus is providing His loving evaluation of each of the seven the churches and telling them what they are doing right or wrong and what they are about to face. He warns and consoles those whom He loves.

At Ephesus, He notes and commends the good deeds they have done but identifies that those good deeds are not the most important thing for them to do. What matters most is that they have left their first love. That is, they are no longer following what they **_first came to believe_**. There was a thorn in their side which needed to be removed.

ACTS 11:1-18 KING JAMES VERSION (KJV)

¹ And the apostles and brethren that were in Judaea heard that the Gentiles had also received the word of God.
² And when Peter was come up to Jerusalem, they that were of the circumcision contended with him,
³ Saying, Thou wentest in to men uncircumcised, and didst eat with them.
⁴ But Peter rehearsed the matter from the beginning, and expounded it by order unto them, saying,
⁵ I was in the city of Joppa praying: and in a trance I saw a vision, A certain vessel descend, as it had been a great sheet, let down from heaven by four corners; and it came even to me:
⁶ Upon the which when I had fastened mine eyes, I considered, and saw fourfooted beasts of the earth, and wild beasts, and creeping things, and fowls of the air.
⁷ And I heard a voice saying unto me, Arise, Peter; slay and eat.

⁸ But I said, Not so, Lord: for nothing common or unclean hath at any time entered into my mouth.
⁹ But the voice answered me again from heaven, What God hath cleansed, that call not thou common.
¹⁰ And this was done three times: and all were drawn up again into heaven.
¹¹ And, behold, immediately there were three men already come unto the house where I was, sent from Caesarea unto me.
¹² And the Spirit bade me go with them, nothing doubting. Moreover these six brethren accompanied me, and we entered into the man's house:
¹³ And he shewed us how he had seen an angel in his house, which stood and said unto him, Send men to Joppa, and call for Simon, whose surname is Peter;
¹⁴ Who shall tell thee words, whereby thou and all thy house shall be saved.
¹⁵ And as I began to speak, the Holy Ghost fell on them, as on us at the beginning.
¹⁶ Then remembered I the word of the Lord, how that he said, John indeed baptized with water; but ye shall be baptized with the Holy Ghost.
¹⁷ Forasmuch then as God gave them the like gift as he did unto us, who believed on the Lord Jesus Christ; what was I, that I could withstand God?
¹⁸ When they heard these things, they held their peace, and glorified God, saying, Then hath God also to the Gentiles granted repentance unto life.

We should note that Jesus uses only a portion of the image presented to John at the beginning of this prophecy in chapter one to describe Himself. He then notes He has the seven stars in His right hand. The right hand with the stars is reminding them that they are not the only Church with which He is communicating. Each star is a leader or angel appointed to lead a particular Church. All these leaders are in His hands, which symbolizes they are under His authority, and belong to Him and are to represent Him. It is also reminding them He is the key to eternal life, which they needed to keep foremost in their minds. He is also pointing to the fact their power comes from Him, not just their efforts. He is indicating that they are His possession, not any other.

The image of Jesus walking among the candlesticks symbolizes that He is interested in their actions and is not far off somewhere else. He is close enough to know what is going on in the body and what they have been doing and what needs to be praised and what needs correction. Not only this, but He is also there to support them. He reminds them of the changes which they have allowed to occur by their response to the Holy Spirit. He points to the fact that there is yet more they need to do. He tells them that there still a need for further repentance from ungodly works. He lets them know it is a matter of extreme importance for them to pay more attention to the work of the Holy Spirit in them, otherwise, they would no longer be allowed to be His representative. They had not arrived at a fully transformed heart of love for God and the brethren. But they had allowed something else to divert their attention from the Holy Spirit. This became the reason for their works. It has been made known to me that what was central to their problem was pride. This is a tool used by the devil. He can easily appeal to man's desire to be wanted and revered or his tendency to allow his selfish nature to dominate his actions.

> **EPHESIANS 2:5-9 EASY-TO-READ VERSION**
>
> *5 We were spiritually dead because of all we had done against him. But he gave us new life together with Christ. (You have been saved by God's grace.)*
>
> *6 Yes, it is because we are a part of Christ Jesus that God raised us from death and seated us together with him in the heavenly places.*
>
> *7 God did this so that his kindness to us who belong to Christ Jesus would clearly show for all time to come the amazing richness of his grace.*
>
> *8 I mean that you have been saved by grace because you believed. You did not save yourselves; it was a gift from God.*
>
> *9 You are not saved by the things you have done, so there is nothing to boast about.*

In this scripture we see the Holy Ghost had been received and had produced what we are all to experience, the fire and power of Jesus surging in us. That is, a change had occurred in them and they came to know that through the sacrifice of Christ Jesus, they received forgiveness of sin, they accepted God as the source of all creation and that by the power of His Spirit they could be able to be transformed in His image, which would produce within them a new heart and a new mind that put God and His righteousness first. This caused them to love God, Jesus, and their brothers and sisters and helped them to be the kingdom of God here on earth. This is the prescribed priority for us all as Christians. It was the need for them to be reborn and to be transformed in His image which was most important, not just doing good works. They needed to keep the goal of Him and His plan to rejuvenate them and release them from the bondage of sin at the forefront of each of their activities. Even though they had accepted this at the beginning, they placed this on hold and started doing things for their own glory. Like most of us, when we see the results of our efforts, we become enamored with our own selves and start to overlook the fact it was God who had placed in us the will to do good works after the fashion in which we were originally created. They had started to turn from glorifying God in what they were accomplishing. It is a fact, a temptation which we all face. We all must realize that everything we do is for His glory and to prove we are the workmanship of His hands. It is a joint accomplishment not ours alone.

He also emphasizes that they needed to be willing to receive His guidance and be willing to follow it. We see the statement "those who have ears to hear" abounds throughout all scripture, indicating it was still our choice either to accept or to reject His instruction. They should have understood from this statement the importance of what was being said.

EPHESIANS 4:17-32 AMPLIFIED BIBLE (AMP)

The Christian's Walk
17 So this I say, and solemnly affirm together with the Lord [as in His presence], that you must no longer live as the [unbelieving] Gentiles live, in the futility of their minds [and in the foolishness and emptiness of their souls],
18 for their [moral] understanding is darkened and their reasoning is clouded; [they are] alienated and self-banished from the life of God [with no share in it; this is] because of the [willful] ignorance and spiritual blindness that is [deep-seated] within them, because of the hardness and insensitivity of their heart.

¹⁹ And they, [the ungodly in their spiritual apathy], having become callous and unfeeling, have given themselves over [as prey] to unbridled sensuality, eagerly craving the practice of every kind of impurity [that their desires may demand].
²⁰ But you did not learn Christ in this way!
²¹ If in fact you have [really] heard Him and have been taught by Him, just as truth is in Jesus [revealed in His life and personified in Him],
²² that, regarding your previous way of life, you put off your old self [completely discard your former nature], which is being corrupted through deceitful desires,
²³ and be continually renewed in the spirit of your mind [having a fresh, untarnished mental and spiritual attitude],
²⁴ and put on the new self [the regenerated and renewed nature], created in God's image, [godlike] in the righteousness and holiness of the truth [living in a way that expresses to God your gratitude for your salvation].
²⁵ Therefore, rejecting all falsehood [whether lying, defrauding, telling half-truths, spreading rumors, any such as these], speak truth each one with his neighbor, for we are all parts of one another [and we are all parts of the body of Christ].
²⁶ Be angry [at sin—at immorality, at injustice, at ungodly behavior], yet do not sin; do not let your anger [cause you shame, nor allow it to] last until the sun goes down.
²⁷ And do not give the devil an opportunity [to lead you into sin by holding a grudge, or nurturing anger, or harboring resentment, or cultivating bitterness].
²⁸ The thief [who has become a believer] must no longer steal, but instead he must work hard [making an honest living], producing that which is good with his own hands, so that he will have something to share with those in need.
²⁹ Do not let unwholesome [foul, profane, worthless, vulgar] words ever come out of your mouth, but only such speech as is good for building up others, according to the need and the occasion, so that it will be a blessing to those who hear [you speak].
³⁰ And do not grieve the Holy Spirit of God [but seek to please Him], by whom you were sealed and marked [branded as God's own] for the day of redemption [the final deliverance from the consequences of sin].
³¹ Let all bitterness and wrath and anger and clamor [perpetual animosity, resentment, strife, fault-finding] and slander be put

away from you, along with every kind of malice [all spitefulness, verbal abuse, malevolence].
³² Be kind and helpful to one another, tender-hearted [compassionate, understanding], forgiving one another [readily and freely], just as God in Christ also forgave [a]you.
Footnotes:
a) Ephesians 4:32 Two early mss read us.

    The center of all activity which we take part in, is our loving God with all our heart mind and strength and loving our neighbors as ourselves. This is how we become one with Him and with each other. Without this level of love, everything we do is worthless and does not matter. Love is the basis of all true Christian activity whether it is directed toward someone else or ourselves. It takes Godly love to truly forgive and forget. It takes Godly love to accept everyone as our true brother or sister or as a mother or father. It takes this same type of love to minister to the need of someone you don't know or have never seen. It takes an ultimate level of love to understand that all that has been provided on earth is for the benefit of all and there should be a proper balance in distributing the wealth God has provided. It takes love to forgive others. Love is needed to accept all that we must face to honor our commitment to Christ and to others. It is love that gives not because someone deserves it, but because it is a gift from God to share liberally just as it has been provided for us. By His power we can achieve the elements of true love which is the same as His and become one with Him and each other.

    It takes Godly love to accept that we are all created equal in Christ Jesus. It takes Godly love to trust that no matter what comes our way, we endure it for the love of our God and fellow saints. It takes Godly love to trust in the fairness of God and accept that Jesus is all we need to be like Him. It takes Godly love to want to be like God and Jesus and to be willing to allow the Holy Spirit to root out all our sinful ways and replace them with the righteous love of God. It takes love to evaluate when others do wrong the need to have that pointed out. It takes Godly love to hate sin and how it can destroy the destiny of an individual. It takes Godly love to have the patience to endure the troubles on this earth, trusting that God will deliver us in the end. It takes Godly love to wait on the resurrection of our bodies so we can enjoy being in His presence for eternity.

Jesus points out that both He and these Christians hate the deeds of the Nicolaitans. Throughout my studies no one has an understanding or seems to have found out what it was the Nicolaitans did. Jesus wants us to understand that there are religious practices which are revolting to Him and that we are to judge these just as He does. Yes, we are to judge wrongdoing.

Not too long ago in a dream the Lord began to show to me what the practice of the Nicolaitans was. He showed me a three-sided chute. This chute was like a box with one open end and no top. It only had three sides. It had a shape such that the closed end was the highest point. Each of these sides sloped downward from the closed end toward the open end. Then there were items which were being placed in it. At first, I could not focus enough to comprehend what these were. It was a blur. At the end of this experience, I was told that what was being placed in this chute were babies, which were being offered up as a sacrifice to some man-made false god.

I know from my studies of the Latin language in high school and from other historic books which I have read in my lifetime that it was not uncommon for people to offer up children as sacrifices. I can recall that it was a customary practice to take unwanted children and place them in the woods for them to die or to be killed by wild animals.

Even in our day and time, in China they limited families to no more than two children and that they also practiced taking unwanted children (those who exceeded the government mandate) and placing them out in the wild to die. The government was also known to mutilate women to prevent them from having children. China had set a limit of one child per family, and which has now increased this to two. I understand they may consider with doing away with this practice altogether since many are aborting female children in favor of males. I understand this government has been receiving increasing protest from countries around the world about this policy. We see worldwide where children are being aborted for the sake of finances, shame, pleasure and other humanistic desires and reasoning. It is a practice which God hates among many others, but He especially hates the shedding of innocent blood. He sees human life as a divine given right which He and only He has the right to determine when it begins and when it ends.

Summary

Let us summarize what there is about Ephesus which is of lasting value. We can see that the letter Paul wrote to them had a profound effect, as they had responded to it and responded to the work of the Holy Spirit. They had let pride in what they did overshadow the purpose behind what they were doing. They had missed what was most important, their spiritual transformation.

1. There had been a move of the Holy Spirit which led them to start doing good works.
2. They needed to reach a new level of love for God and each other but somehow, they lost insight into this.
3. They had gained the knowledge of that which is evil in the sight of God and they did not tolerate it among them.
4. They had gained enough knowledge to be able to spot false doctrine and those who promoted it. This came through studying scripture under the tutelage of the Holy Spirit, they were able to identify what was false teaching just as Jesus did when confronted by the twisted interpretation of scripture by the devil at the end of His forty day fast.

> **Matthew 7:10-16 Amplified Bible**
> **10** *Or if he asks for a fish, will [instead] give him a snake?*
> **11** *If you then, evil (sinful by nature) as you are, know how to give good and advantageous gifts to your children, how much more will your Father who is in heaven [perfect as He is] give what is good and advantageous to those who keep on asking Him.*
> **12** *"So then, in everything treat others the same way you want them to treat you, for this is [the essence of] the Law and the [writings of the] Prophets.*
> **The Narrow and Wide Gates**
> **13** *"Enter through the narrow gate. For wide is the gate and broad and easy to travel is the path that leads the way to destruction and eternal loss, and there are many who enter through it.*
> **14** *But small is the gate and narrow and difficult to travel is the path that leads the way to [everlasting] life, and there are few who find it.*
> **A Tree and Its Fruit**

> [15] "Beware of the false prophets, [teachers] who come to you dressed as sheep [appearing gentle and innocent], but inwardly are ravenous wolves.
> [16] By their fruit you will recognize them [that is, by their contrived doctrine and self-focus]. Do people pick grapes from thorn bushes or figs from thistles?

5. They understood doctrines which were evil and learned to hate them as Jesus did. They were converted to the point they had an understanding of religious practices which are born of evil (the devil).

> **2 Timothy 4:2-4 King James Version (KJV)**
> [2] *Preach the word; be instant in season, out of season; reprove, rebuke, exhort with all long suffering and doctrine.*
> [3] *For the time will come when they will not endure sound doctrine; but after their own lusts shall they heap to themselves teachers, having itching ears;*
> [4] *And they shall turn away their ears from the truth, and shall be turned unto fables.*

6. They were operating ignoring their need to wait upon the Lord and the need to be willing to persevere as long as needed.
7. They had stopped doing what was their first love; which was to be reborn and to spread the work of the cross, the crucifixion and the offer of eternal life to those who were willing to repent.

These are the eternal truths which we are to gain from this book.

1. Do good works designed by God. Scripture contains these in many forms and actions. Paul outlines most of these in His letter to the Ephesians years prior to the presentation of this prophecy. The beginning and ending of our good works should be to glorify God and Christ Jesus.
2. All that we do should be driven by our love for God and our fellowman.
3. Hate evil and those who promote it. Scripture provides instances which guide us into understanding how these are implemented. Prayerfully read these as presented in the letter to the Ephesians by Paul.

4. Study the scripture and allow the Holy Spirit to teach you to be knowledgeable of what God hates and loves so that we can be able to identify these.
5. Study the scripture and allow the Holy Spirit to teach you the difference between false doctrine and correct doctrine and how to spot phonies claiming to be of Christ.
6. Be fervent in proclaiming the gospel of Christ and His call to repentance and the offer of the gift of eternal life.
7. If we are willing, He will bring us understanding. Those Churches which have ears to hear let them hear. Note the expression here in Revelation 2:7 clearly designates that it is a message to every Church then and now and in the future. What is being said is for every Church to learn.

Revelation 2:7 King James Version (KJV)
⁷ He that hath an ear, let him hear what the Spirit saith unto the Churches; To him that overcometh will I give to eat of the tree of life, which is in the midst of the paradise of God.

8. They were being called to establish the highest level of response to His work in them.
9. Seek first the kingdom which is the love of God and our brothers and sisters. Be fervent in proclaiming this by your lifestyle and through your actions in order that others might be freed from the bondage of sin and join us in eternity.
10. Walk in the light of the Spirit to be able to repent from dead works and be converted to the righteous works.
11. Heed the admonition of the ministers **who are called** to lead the Churches in the right path. Ministers are called to minister in righteousness. **Prove the false ministers as liars.**
12. Be alert to the instruction of Christ provided through the gift of prophecy.
13. **Beware of those who claim to be prophets but who are not called of God.**
14. **Don't let pride overcome you.**

CHAPTER 4

Grace and What it Means.

EPHESIANS 1:4-16 KING JAMES VERSION

⁴ According as he hath chosen us in him before the foundation of the world, that we should be holy and without blame before him in love:
⁵ Having predestinated us unto the adoption of children by Jesus Christ to himself, according to the good pleasure of his will,
⁶ To the praise of the glory of his grace, wherein he hath made us accepted in the beloved.
⁷ In whom we have redemption through his blood, the forgiveness of sins, according to the riches of his grace;
⁸ Wherein he hath abounded toward us in all wisdom and prudence;
⁹ Having made known unto us the mystery of his will, according to his good pleasure which he hath purposed in himself:
¹⁰ That in the dispensation of the fulness of times he might gather together in one all things in Christ, both which are in heaven, and which are on earth; even in him:
¹¹ In whom also we have obtained an inheritance, being predestinated according to the purpose of him who worketh all things after the counsel of his own will:
¹² That we should be to the praise of his glory, who first trusted in Christ.
¹³ In whom ye also trusted, after that ye heard the word of truth, the gospel of your salvation: in whom also after that ye believed, ye were sealed with that holy Spirit of promise,
¹⁴ Which is the earnest of our inheritance until the redemption of the purchased possession, unto the praise of his glory.

¹⁵ *Wherefore I also, after I heard of your faith in the Lord Jesus, and love unto all the saints,*
¹⁶ *Cease not to give thanks for you, making mention of you in my prayers;*

GALATIANS 3:26-29 KING JAMES VERSION

²⁶ *For ye are all the children of God by faith in Christ Jesus.*
²⁷ *For as many of you as have been baptized into Christ have put on Christ.*
²⁸ *There is neither Jew nor Greek, there is neither bond nor free, there is neither male nor female: for ye are all one in Christ Jesus.*
²⁹ *And if ye be Christ's, then are ye Abraham's seed, and heirs according to the promise.*

GALATIANS 3:26-29 EASY-TO-READ VERSION

²⁶⁻²⁷ *You were all baptized into Christ, and so you were all clothed with Christ. This shows that you are all children of God through faith in Christ Jesus.*
²⁸ *Now, in Christ, it doesn't matter if you are a Jew or a Greek, a slave or free, male or female. You are all the same in Christ Jesus.*
²⁹ *You belong to Christ, so you are Abraham's descendants. You get all of God's blessings because of the promise that God made to Abraham.*

If we look into this we find major insights into what is the essential meaning is of grace and the what, how, where, and when of grace. We should take note that grace is defined in scripture as being created by God and is implemented in us through Jesus and the Holy Spirit. Each step in the Christian's walk is initiated by God. So each part of our acceptance of Jesus including the act of repentance, the desire to do the good works were created to do all the way to the work of transforming us from our sin nature to the final stage of perfecting us to dwell with God in heavenly places, is His doing. It is God who performs this work in us not us doing it on our own. Review this again.

EPHESIANS 2:4-6 KING JAMES VERSION

⁴ *But God, who is rich in mercy, for his great love wherewith he loved us,*
⁵ *Even when we were dead in sins, hath quickened us together with Christ, (by grace ye are saved;)*

⁶ And hath raised us up together, and made us sit together in heavenly places in Christ Jesus:

JOHN 1:15-17 KING JAMES VERSION

¹⁵ John bare witness of him, and cried, saying, This was he of whom I spake, He that cometh after me is preferred before me: for he was before me.
¹⁶ And of his fulness have all we received, and grace for grace.
¹⁷ For the law was given by Moses, but grace and truth came by Jesus Christ.

ACTS 15:5-12 EASY-TO-READ VERSION

⁵ Some of the believers in Jerusalem had belonged to the Pharisees. They stood up and said, "The non-Jewish believers must be circumcised. We must tell them to obey the Law of Moses!"
⁶ Then the apostles and the elders gathered to study this problem.
⁷ After a long debate, Peter stood up and said to them, "My brothers, I am sure you remember what happened in the early days. God chose me from among you to tell the Good News to those who are not Jewish. It was from me that they heard the Good News and believed.
⁸ God knows everyone, even their thoughts, and he accepted these non-Jewish people. He showed this to us by giving them the Holy Spirit the same as he did to us.
⁹ To God, those people are not different from us. When they believed, God made their hearts pure.
10 So now, why are you putting a heavy burden[a] around the necks of the non-Jewish followers of Jesus? Are you trying to make God angry? We and our fathers were not able to carry that burden. ¹¹ No, we believe that we and these people will be saved the same way—by the grace of the Lord Jesus."
¹² Then the whole group became quiet. They listened while Paul and Barnabas told about all the miraculous signs and wonders that God had done through them among the non-Jewish people.
 Footnotes
  a) Acts 15:10 burden The Jewish law. Some of the Jews tried to make the non-Jewish believers follow this law.

The work of grace all starts with God the father and is realized for us in Jesus. God planned this from the very beginning that Jesus should be the source for us to receive this grace and for us to flourish in it. God states here that for His plan of grace to be implemented we must receive it through Jesus. Grace is the full expression of God's love to us. It is the path that we need to arrive at to be acceptable at the last day. So, grace can only be granted not earned. This grace sole intent is granted for us to be made Holy and righteous. So, the source starts with God's love for His creation and is sourced through Jesus and put into action by Him. Without God and Jesus there is no grace in the life of man. It can only be expressed by our acceptance of Jesus as its implementer and all we can do is open ourselves and others to receive it by our adherence to the call to be Holy and righteous.

ACTS 20:31-32 EASY-TO-READ VERSION

31 So be careful! And always remember what I did during the three years I was with you. I never stopped reminding each one of you how you should live, counseling you day and night and crying over you.

32 "Now I am putting you in God's care. I am depending on the message about his grace to make you strong. That message is able to give you the blessings that God gives to all his holy people.

JOHN 8:41-43 EASY-TO-READ VERSION

41 So you are doing what your own father did."
But they said, "We are not like children who never knew who their father was. God is our Father. He is the only Father we have."
42 Jesus said to them, "If God were really your Father, you would love me. I came from God, and now I am here. I did not come by my own authority. God sent me.
43 You don't understand the things I say, because you cannot accept my teaching.

JOHN 14:14-16 EASY-TO-READ VERSION

14 If you ask me for anything in my name, I will do it.
The Promise of the Holy Spirit
15 "If you love me, you will do what I command. 16 I will ask the Father, and he will give you another Helper[a] to be with you forever.

Footnotes
John 14:16 Helper Or "Comforter," the Holy Spirit (see "Holy Spirit" in the Word List). Also in verse 26.

JOHN 14:22-30 EASY-TO-READ VERSION

²² Then Judas (not Judas Iscariot) said, "Lord, how will you make yourself known to us, but not to the world?"
²³ Jesus answered, "All who love me will obey my teaching. My Father will love them. My Father and I will come to them and live with them. ²⁴ But anyone who does not love me does not obey my teaching. This teaching that you hear is not really mine. It is from my Father who sent me.
²⁵ "I have told you all these things while I am with you.
²⁶ But the Helper will teach you everything and cause you to remember all that I told you. This Helper is the Holy Spirit that the Father will send in my name.
²⁷ "I leave you peace. It is my own peace I give you. I give you peace in a different way than the world does. So don't be troubled. Don't be afraid.
²⁸ You heard me say to you, 'I am leaving, but I will come back to you.' If you loved me, you would be happy that I am going back to the Father, because the Father is greater than I am.
²⁹ I have told you this now, before it happens. Then when it happens, you will believe.
³⁰ "I will not talk with you much longer. The ruler of this world is coming. He has no power over me.

This is tough to handle since our part is the role of being a receiver. We cannot earn it, nor do we deserve it. It is an act which was foreordained by God the Father and that is it. God the Father set the rules and that is it. Grace then is a Holy expression of the love of God toward us. It is freely given based on the work of Jesus not ours. Now as I speak It being freely provided, I should back up. The purpose of God is to set us free from the human condition which is our lustfulness which is full of sinful acts. So freely does not mean there are not conditions which have to be met. Jesus and the father preordained the plan of salvation which is expressed as His loving grace. Wait, is this double talk? No, it is not. Let us examine this a little further. Look again at Jesus rebuke of the Ephesians provided in the book of revelation.

REVELATION 2 EASY-TO-READ VERSION

Jesus' Letter to the Church in Ephesus
¹ "Write this to the angel of the church in Ephesus:

> "Here is a message from the one who holds the seven stars in his right hand and walks among the seven golden lampstands.
> ² "I know what you do, how hard you work and never give up. I know that you don't accept evil people. You have tested those who say they are apostles but are not. You found that they are liars.
> ³ You never stop trying. You have endured troubles for my name and have not given up.
> ⁴ "But I have this against you: You have left the love you had in the beginning.
> ⁵ So remember where you were before you fell. Change your hearts and do what you did at first. If you don't change, I will come to you and remove your lampstand from its place.
> ⁶ But there is something you do that is right—you hate the things that the Nicolaitans[a] do. I also hate what they do.
> ⁷ "Everyone who hears this should listen to what the Spirit says to the churches. To those who win the victory I will give the right to eat the fruit from the tree of life, which is in God's paradise.

Again, see how Christ commends their hard work and the deeds which they are doing but their focus was on the wrong thing. They did not continue to accept that the source of the good they did was Jesus not their own efforts. It is our faith in Him and trust in Him which brings about the change needed to carry us to perfection. The analogy is He is carrying us through the muck and mire of this world on to something much better.

We must choose to accept the terms attached to receive this grace. Again, see the admonition provided by Jesus Himself.

> ### JOHN 14:22-30 EASY-TO-READ VERSION
> ²² Then Judas (not Judas Iscariot) said, "Lord, how will you make yourself known to us, but not to the world?"
> ²³ Jesus answered, "All who love me will obey my teaching. My Father will love them. My Father and I will come to them and live with them. ²⁴ But anyone who does not love me does not obey my teaching. This teaching that you hear is not really mine. It is from my Father who sent me.
> ²⁵ "I have told you all these things while I am with you.
> ²⁶ But the Helper will teach you everything and cause you to remember all that I told you. This Helper is the Holy Spirit that the Father will send in my name.

> [27] *"I leave you peace. It is my own peace I give you. I give you peace in a different way than the world does. So don't be troubled. Don't be afraid.*
> [28] *You heard me say to you, 'I am leaving, but I will come back to you.' If you loved me, you would be happy that I am going back to the Father, because the Father is greater than I am.*
> [29] *I have told you this now, before it happens. Then when it happens, you will believe.*
> [30] *"I will not talk with you much longer. The ruler of this world is coming. He has no power over me.*

Yes, even though it is free it is not without terms and conditions. Like any contract we agree to its terms. This is a contract which we make with God. The provisions of this contract are that we need to repent and submit to being reborn by allowing the process of regrowth under the tutorship of Jesus through the work of the Holy Spirit. It does not mean that we give up being who we are but it means we learn the way of sin is death and the sinful acts which we have acquired are shown for what they are and we become free to be released from their hold on our lives. When given permission Jesus through the Holy Spirit works to provide us with the will to resist the sin in our lives and then we can allow the Holy Spirit to make the necessary adjustments so that we choose to be righteous and no longer held in the bonds of sinful conduct. When this occurs, we become made new and the work of the Holy Spirit can help cement righteousness within us. This is grace at work. God accepts the role of removing sinful conduct from within us and can make us acceptable through the transforming work which brings us to the point of being Holy and righteous. Then we can meet the provisions necessary to dwell in His presence. Our role in the process of grace is described as this; a state of being not doing.

God and Jesus use the Holy Spirit to cement in us His offer of grace. He does this when He sees we are prepared to receive this. Only He can determine this. I know we feel that we have had something which has caused us to find God. It is He who initiated this process when He sees the time is right. The correct viewpoint is I once was lost but now I am found. He does not desire that any should perish but at the same time He will not force us into this. We must make this choice freely.

2 PETER 3:8-10 EASY-TO-READ VERSION

⁸ But don't forget this one thing, dear friends: To the Lord a day is like a thousand years, and a thousand years is like a day.
⁹ The Lord is not being slow in doing what he promised—the way some people understand slowness. But God is being patient with you. He doesn't want anyone to be lost. He wants everyone to change their ways and stop sinning.
¹⁰ But the day when the Lord comes again will surprise everyone like the coming of a thief. The sky will disappear with a loud noise. Everything in the sky will be destroyed with fire. And the earth and everything in it will be burned up.[a]

Footnotes
a) 2 Peter 3:10 will be burned up Among the other readings of this text in early Greek copies, many have "will be found," and one has "will disappear."

Let us examine one instance from scripture. It is the experience of Paul on the road to Damascus.

ACTS 9:1-25 EASY-TO-READ VERSION

Saul Becomes a Follower of Jesus
⁹ In Jerusalem Saul was still trying to scare the followers of the Lord, even saying he would kill them. He went to the high priest
² and asked him to write letters to the synagogues in the city of Damascus. Saul wanted the high priest to give him the authority to find people in Damascus who were followers of the Way. If he found any believers there, men or women, he would arrest them and bring them back to Jerusalem.
³ So Saul went to Damascus. When he came near the city, a very bright light from heaven suddenly shined around him.
⁴ He fell to the ground and heard a voice saying to him, "Saul, Saul! Why are you persecuting me?"
⁵ Saul said, "Who are you, Lord?"
The voice answered, "I am Jesus, the one you are persecuting.
⁶ Get up now and go into the city. Someone there will tell you what you must do."
⁷ The men traveling with Saul just stood there, unable to speak. They heard the voice, but they saw no one
⁸ Saul got up from the ground and opened his eyes, but he could not see. So the men with him held his hand and led him into Damascus. ⁹ For three days, Saul could not see; he did not eat or drink.

¹⁰ There was a follower of Jesus in Damascus named Ananias. In a vision the Lord said to him, "Ananias!"
Ananias answered, "Here I am, Lord."
¹¹ The Lord said to him, "Get up and go to the street called Straight Street. Find the house of Judas[a] and ask for a man named Saul from the city of Tarsus. He is there now, praying.
¹² He has seen a vision in which a man named Ananias came and laid his hands on him so that he could see again."
¹³ But Ananias answered, "Lord, many people have told me about this man. They told me about the many bad things he did to your holy people in Jerusalem.
¹⁴ Now he has come here to Damascus. The leading priests have given him the power to arrest all people who trust in you.[b]"
¹⁵ But the Lord Jesus said to Ananias, "Go! I have chosen Saul for an important work. I want him to tell other nations, their rulers, and the people of Israel about me.
¹⁶ I will show him all that he must suffer for me."
¹⁷ So Ananias left and went to the house of Judas. He laid his hands on Saul and said, "Saul, my brother, the Lord Jesus sent me. He is the one you saw on the road when you came here. He sent me so that you can see again and also be filled with the Holy Spirit."
¹⁸ Immediately, something that looked like fish scales fell off Saul's eyes. He was able to see! Then he got up and was baptized.
¹⁹ After he ate, he began to feel strong again.

Saul Begins to Tell About Jesus

Saul stayed with the followers of Jesus in Damascus for a few days. ²⁰ Soon he began to go to the synagogues and tell people about Jesus. He told the people, "Jesus is the Son of God!"
²¹ All the people who heard Saul were amazed. They said, "This is the same man who was in Jerusalem trying to destroy the people who trust in Jesus[c]! And that's why he has come here—to arrest the followers of Jesus and take them back to the leading priests."
²² But Saul became more and more powerful in proving that Jesus is the Messiah. His proofs were so strong that the Jews who lived in Damascus could not argue with him.

Saul Escapes From Some Jews

²³ After many days, some Jews made plans to kill Saul.
²⁴ They were watching the city gates day and night. They wanted to kill Saul, but he learned about their plan.

²⁵ One night some followers that Saul had taught helped him leave the city. They put him in a basket and lowered it down through a hole in the city wall.
   Footnotes
   a) *Acts 9:11 Judas This is not either of the apostles named Judas.*
   b) *Acts 9:14 who trust in you Literally, "who call on your name," meaning to show faith in Jesus by worshiping him or praying to him for help.*

ACTS 9:21 WHO TRUST IN JESUS LITERALLY, "WHO CALL ON THIS NAME."

REVELATION 2:19-21 KING JAMES VERSION

¹⁹ I know thy works, and charity, and service, and faith, and thy patience, and thy works; and the last to be more than the first.
²⁰ Notwithstanding I have a few things against thee, because thou sufferest that woman Jezebel, which calleth herself a prophetess, to teach and to seduce my servants to commit fornication, and to eat things sacrificed unto idols.
²¹ And I gave her space to repent of her fornication; and she repented not.

Here you can see the hand of the Lord at work. He was able to determine now was the time which Paul was ready for conversion. This is unlike Jezebel in the book of Revelation whom the Lord had provided time for her to repent but she refused to respond positively. Not so with Paul, for Paul this was a life changing experience. The grace of Lord was initiated in Paul and it was this grace which convinced him to repent and change the course of his life and become a minister apostle appointed to spread the good news of grace to all who were willing to receive it. Even though we may see Paul as being forced into this by being made blind the final choice was his to make. Paul's blindness opened his eyes and ears to hear and understand things which he was blind to when he had sight.

Summary

We can see here it is the Lord's plan to provide an escape route from our sin for all who are willing to receive His gift of salvation which includes.

- Our Choice to accept his offer of salvation through Jesus.
- The recognition in us that we are sinful and repentance is needed.
- The agreement we will allow the Lord to transform us from sinful ways by the influence of the Holy Spirit.
- We are provided the gift of the Holy Spirit which implants righteousness in us and which encourages us to perform the good works for which we were originally created.
- The gift of the Holy Spirit to expose our sinful ways and to be freed from their influence.
- The Holy Spirit guiding us into all truth.
- Finally providing the perfection so that we can dwell in the presence of Father God.
- This is all God's doing with our eye-opening experience.

We see this in scripture and in every act of the work of the Lord. We can see from scripture and our life experience that not every Christian receives the entirety of grace all at once and we continue to function based on our sinful nature. Paul did not immediately become patient as can be seen with his journeys and dealings with others who were with him. We can also see this in the reluctance of Ananias to accept the instruction to go to Paul and the group who plotted to kill him, yet others reacted to the grace of God and protected Paul. So, all that we are and all that we will become and do is the result of His grace not our effort. Yes, it takes effort to do good works but the will and encouragement and true initiative (Godly Love) are from Him. This is so no man can boast that he has done this in and of himself. He is the author and finisher of our faith and all that it takes for us to be freed from our sinful state.

ROMANS 3:26-28 AMPLIFIED BIBLE

[26] It was to demonstrate His righteousness at the present time, so that He would be just and the One who justifies those who have faith in Jesus [and rely confidently on Him as Savior].

²⁷ Then what becomes of [our] boasting? It is excluded [entirely ruled out, banished]. On what principle? On [the principle of good] works? No, but on the principle of faith.
²⁸ For we maintain that an individual is justified by faith distinctly apart from works of the Law [the observance of which has nothing to do with justification, that is, being declared free of the guilt of sin and made acceptable to God].

EPHESIANS 2:8-10 EASY-TO-READ VERSION

⁸ I mean that you have been saved by grace because you believed. You did not save yourselves; it was a gift from God.
⁹ You are not saved by the things you have done, so there is nothing to boast about.
¹⁰ God has made us what we are. In Christ Jesus, God made us new people so that we would spend our lives doing the good things he had already planned for us to do.

We can see even in the Old Testament there was understanding of grace when David repents of his sin in Psalm 51. He admits his sin and then asks for forgiveness because he knows the grace of God is always there. Then there is the time when the Lord had to remind Paul of his grace. Yes, even Paul had to be reminded it is God's grace which brings salvation and no weapon the devil throws at us will prosper. It is by grace we are saved and that is a done deal. The only way for us to lose his favor or grace is for us to refuse to accept it. Even when the Ephesians were told in the book of Revelation that their candlestick could be replaced, we see no mention of them losing the grace provided in Jesus for their salvation. It is just that the choices they were making stood in the way of His plan being completed. Review these points in the scripture below.

PSALM 51:1-12 KING JAMES VERSION

¹ Have mercy upon me, O God, according to thy lovingkindness: according unto the multitude of thy tender mercies blot out my transgressions.
² Wash me throughly from mine iniquity, and cleanse me from my sin.
³ For I acknowledge my transgressions: and my sin is ever before me.

⁴ Against thee, thee only, have I sinned, and done this evil in thy sight: that thou mightest be justified when thou speakest, and be clear when thou judgest.
⁵ Behold, I was shapen in iniquity; and in sin did my mother conceive me.
⁶ Behold, thou desirest truth in the inward parts: and in the hidden part thou shalt make me to know wisdom.
⁷ Purge me with hyssop, and I shall be clean: wash me, and I shall be whiter than snow.
⁸ Make me to hear joy and gladness; that the bones which thou hast broken may rejoice.
⁹ Hide thy face from my sins, and blot out all mine iniquities.
¹⁰ Create in me a clean heart, O God; and renew a right spirit within me.
¹¹ Cast me not away from thy presence; and take not thy holy spirit from me.
¹² Restore unto me the joy of thy salvation; and uphold me with thy free spirit.

2 Corinthians 12:6-9 Amplified Bible
⁶ If I wish to boast, I will not be foolish, because I will be speaking the truth. But I abstain [from it], so that no one will credit me with more than [is justified by what] he sees in me or hears from me.
A Thorn in the Flesh
⁷ Because of the surpassing greatness and extraordinary nature of the revelations [which I received from God], for this reason, to keep me from thinking of myself as important, a thorn in the flesh was given to me, a messenger of Satan, to torment and harass me—to keep me from exalting myself!
⁸ Concerning this I pleaded with the Lord three times that it might leave me;
⁹ but He has said to me, "My grace is sufficient for you [My lovingkindness and My mercy are more than enough—always available—regardless of the situation]; for [My] power is being perfected [and is completed and shows itself most effectively] in [your] weakness." Therefore, I will all the more gladly boast in my weaknesses, so that the power of Christ [may completely enfold me and] may dwell in me.

REVELATION 2:1-7 EASY-TO-READ VERSION

Jesus' Letter to the Church in Ephesus
¹ "Write this to the angel of the church in Ephesus:

"Here is a message from the one who holds the seven stars in his right hand and walks among the seven golden lampstands.

2 "I know what you do, how hard you work and never give up. I know that you don't accept evil people. You have tested those who say they are apostles but are not. You found that they are liars.

3 You never stop trying. You have endured troubles for my name and have not given up.

4 "But I have this against you: You have left the love you had in the beginning.

5 So remember where you were before you fell. Change your hearts and do what you did at first. If you don't change, I will come to you and remove your lampstand from its place.

6 But there is something you do that is right—you hate the things that the Nicolaitans[a] do. I also hate what they do.

7 "Everyone who hears this should listen to what the Spirit says to the churches. To those who win the victory I will give the right to eat the fruit from the tree of life, which is in God's paradise.

Footnotes
a) Revelation 2:6 Nicolaitans A religious group that followed wrong ideas. Also in verse 15.

JOHN 9:1-38 KING JAMES VERSION (KJV)

1 And as Jesus passed by, he saw a man which was blind from his birth.

2 And his disciples asked him, saying, Master, who did sin, this man, or his parents, that he was born blind?

3 Jesus answered, Neither hath this man sinned, nor his parents: but that the works of God should be made manifest in him.

4 I must work the works of him that sent me, while it is day: the night cometh, when no man can work.

5 As long as I am in the world, I am the light of the world.

6 When he had thus spoken, he spat on the ground, and made clay of the spittle, and he anointed the eyes of the blind man with the clay,

7 And said unto him, Go, wash in the pool of Siloam, (which is by interpretation, Sent.) He went his way therefore, and washed, and came seeing.

8 The neighbours therefore, and they which before had seen him that he was blind, said, Is not this he that sat and begged?

9 Some said, This is he: others said, He is like him: but he said, I am he.

¹⁰ *Therefore said they unto him, How were thine eyes opened?*
¹¹ *He answered and said, A man that is called Jesus made clay, and anointed mine eyes, and said unto me, Go to the pool of Siloam, and wash: and I went and washed, and I received sight.*
¹² *Then said they unto him, Where is he? He said, I know not.*
¹³ *They brought to the Pharisees him that aforetime was blind.*
¹⁴ *And it was the sabbath day when Jesus made the clay, and opened his eyes.*
¹⁵ *Then again the Pharisees also asked him how he had received his sight. He said unto them, He put clay upon mine eyes, and I washed, and do see.*
¹⁶ *Therefore said some of the Pharisees, This man is not of God, because he keepeth not the sabbath day. Others said, How can a man that is a sinner do such miracles? And there was a division among them.*
¹⁷ *They say unto the blind man again, What sayest thou of him, that he hath opened thine eyes? He said, He is a prophet.*
¹⁸ *But the Jews did not believe concerning him, that he had been blind, and received his sight, until they called the parents of him that had received his sight.*
¹⁹ *And they asked them, saying, Is this your son, who ye say was born blind? how then doth he now see?*
²⁰ *His parents answered them and said, We know that this is our son, and that he was born blind:*
²¹ *But by what means he now seeth, we know not; or who hath opened his eyes, we know not: he is of age; ask him: he shall speak for himself.*
²² *These words spake his parents, because they feared the Jews: for the Jews had agreed already, that if any man did confess that he was Christ, he should be put out of the synagogue.*
²³ *Therefore said his parents, He is of age; ask him.*
²⁴ *Then again called they the man that was blind, and said unto him, Give God the praise: we know that this man is a sinner.*
²⁵ *He answered and said, Whether he be a sinner or no, I know not: one thing I know, that, whereas I was blind, now I see.*
²⁶ *Then said they to him again, What did he to thee? how opened he thine eyes?*
²⁷ *He answered them, I have told you already, and ye did not hear: wherefore would ye hear it again? will ye also be his disciples?*
²⁸ *Then they reviled him, and said, Thou art his disciple; but we are Moses' disciples.*

²⁹ We know that God spake unto Moses: as for this fellow, we know not from whence he is.
³⁰ The man answered and said unto them, Why herein is a marvellous thing, that ye know not from whence he is, and yet he hath opened mine eyes.
³¹ Now we know that God heareth not sinners: but if any man be a worshipper of God, and doeth his will, him he heareth.
³² Since the world began was it not heard that any man opened the eyes of one that was born blind.
³³ If this man were not of God, he could do nothing.
³⁴ They answered and said unto him, Thou wast altogether born in sins, and dost thou teach us? And they cast him out.
³⁵ Jesus heard that they had cast him out; and when he had found him, he said unto him, Dost thou believe on the Son of God?
³⁶ He answered and said, Who is he, Lord, that I might believe on him?
³⁷ And Jesus said unto him, Thou hast both seen him, and it is he that talketh with thee.
³⁸ And he said, Lord, I believe. And he worshipped him.

We can see that salvation is conditional even though the love of God is unconditional. Salvation is given freely but it is based on a set of conditions which we are required to obey. This obedience is based on our loving as God loves. We are provided freedom from the ultimate payment for our sinful conduct along with the promise God Himself will perfect us through the work of Jesus who through the Holy Spirit guides us into all truth and helps us fulfill the fact for which we were created. This is to perform good works (works initiated out of Godly love not duty or self-will). It is through the work of God the Father, Jesus, and the Holy Spirit that we can become one in them and each other and perform the good works for which we were created by God to do. It is not that we are inherently good but that we are just the opposite. We are inherently evil. This will be discussed more in the following chapters.

EPHESIANS 2:4-8 EASY-TO-READ VERSION

⁴ But God is rich in mercy, and he loved us very much.
⁵ We were spiritually dead because of all we had done against him. But he gave us new life together with Christ. (You have been saved by God's grace.)

⁶ Yes, it is because we are a part of Christ Jesus that God raised us from death and seated us together with him in the heavenly places.
⁷ God did this so that his kindness to us who belong to Christ Jesus would clearly show for all time to come the amazing richness of his grace.
⁸ I mean that you have been saved by grace because you believed. You did not save yourselves; it was a gift from God.

CHAPTER 5

Good Works, How They Become A Driving Force in Us

EPHESIANS 2:1-8 EASY-TO-READ VERSION

From Death to Life
¹ In the past you were spiritually dead because of your sins and the things you did against God.
² Yes, in the past your lives were full of those sins. You lived the way the world lives, following the ruler of the evil powers[a] that are above the earth. That same spirit is now working in those who refuse to obey God.
³ In the past all of us lived like that, trying to please our sinful selves. We did all the things our bodies and minds wanted. Like everyone else in the world, we deserved to suffer God's anger just because of the way we were.
⁴ But God is rich in mercy, and he loved us very much.
⁵ We were spiritually dead because of all we had done against him. But he gave us new life together with Christ. (You have been saved by God's grace.)
⁶ Yes, it is because we are a part of Christ Jesus that God raised us from death and seated us together with him in the heavenly places.
⁷ God did this so that his kindness to us who belong to Christ Jesus would clearly show for all time to come the amazing richness of his grace.
⁸ I mean that you have been saved by grace because you believed. You did not save yourselves; it was a gift from God.
   Footnotes

a) *Ephesians 2:2 ruler of the evil powers See "Satan" in the Word List*

1 JOHN 3:18 KING JAMES VERSION

¹⁸ My little children, let us not love in word, neither in tongue; but in deed and in truth.

1 JOHN 3:18 EASY-TO-READ VERSION

¹⁸ My children, our love should not be only words and talk. No, our love must be real. We must show our love by the things we do.

We can see from the quoted text that all human beings are considered sinful by God until we accept the free gift of salvation. It is the work of God which initiates the motivations behind all that we do whenever we truly repent and become obedient to the instruction of the Holy Spirit. Examine this scripture carefully because for many it is difficult to accept the fact that we are sinful. No, we label immoral behavior in others and possible problem areas within ourselves but we do not want to call it sin. We shy away from the concept of sin. For most it is not politically correct to label us as sinful. Yet is a state provided us from the Lord God. We try to avoid it, but we cannot in the sight of God. Look at the list provided in this scripture in Ephesians 2 quoted above. It lists things which God labels as the basis of sinful conduct. First it labels us as followers of the evil one (evil powers of the air). God identifies the first part of our sinful conduct is that we follow the works of Satan. Yes, the Lord identifies all who are not true believers as followers of Satan's influence. If you were to say this to the average person on the street, do you think they would say you are right or that this scripture is accurately translated. I know for me myself it was a revelation to read this and accept it. I cannot place myself in a role such as this, but God has grouped us into this mold. Most are unaware of the fact we are either followers of God or followers of the prince of the power of the air or kingdom of the air, Satan. No that just can't be, but folks this is what God presents to us. We must come to accept that before we accepted Jesus as our savior the world and all its attributes which we highly esteem are the way of Satan. So, we are partakers of the world in which we live and its ruler Satan.

ISAIAH 5:19-21 KING JAMES VERSION

¹⁹ That say, Let him make speed, and hasten his work, that we may see it: and let the counsel of the Holy One of Israel draw nigh and come, that we may know it!
²⁰ Woe unto them that call evil good, and good evil; that put darkness for light, and light for darkness; that put bitter for sweet, and sweet for bitter!
²¹ Woe unto them that are wise in their own eyes, and prudent in their own sight!

EPHESIANS 6:11-13 KING JAMES VERSION

¹¹ Put on the whole armour of God, that ye may be able to stand against the wiles of the devil.
¹² For we wrestle not against flesh and blood, but against principalities, against powers, against the rulers of the darkness of this world, against spiritual wickedness in high places.
¹³ Wherefore take unto you the whole armour of God, that ye may be able to withstand in the evil day, and having done all, to stand.

EPHESIANS 6:11-13 AMPLIFIED BIBLE

¹¹ Put on the full armor of God [for His precepts are like the splendid armor of a heavily-armed soldier], so that you may be able to [successfully] stand up against all the schemes and the strategies and the deceits of the devil.
¹² For our struggle is not against flesh and blood [contending only with physical opponents], but against the rulers, against the powers, against the world forces of this [present] darkness, against the spiritual forces of wickedness in the heavenly (supernatural) places.
¹³ Therefore, put on the complete armor of God, so that you will be able to [successfully] resist and stand your ground in the evil day [of danger], and having done everything [that the crisis demands], to stand firm [in your place, fully prepared, immovable, victorious].

EPHESIANS 6:11-13 EASY-TO-READ VERSION

¹¹ Wear the full armor of God. Wear God's armor so that you can fight against the devil's clever tricks.
¹² Our fight is not against people on earth. We are fighting against the rulers and authorities and the powers of this world's darkness.

We are fighting against the spiritual powers of evil in the heavenly places.
¹³ That is why you need to get God's full armor. Then on the day of evil, you will be able to stand strong. And when you have finished the whole fight, you will still be standing.

PSALM 14:1-3 AMPLIFIED BIBLE

Folly and Wickedness of Men.
To the Chief Musician. A Psalm of David.
¹ The [spiritually ignorant] fool has said in his heart, "There is no God."
They are corrupt, they have committed repulsive and unspeakable deeds;
There is no one who does good.
² The Lord has looked down from heaven upon the children of men
To see if there are any who understand (act wisely),
Who [truly] seek after God, [longing for His wisdom and guidance].
³ They have all turned aside, together they have become corrupt;
There is no one who does good, not even one.

I can easily recall the words of my parents which resound so often. These were "we want you to have it better than what we had." So, I took it to mean that they wanted me to have a richer lifestyle and bigger house and cars and more money and more comfort. This is the way of the world more, more money and more things and more prestige more for me and the heck with others. Yes, it is about me, my, and mine. My understanding of what they told me was far from their intent.

Oh, did I fail to mention that the Lord labels us as disobedient. Well so many will say disobedient to what? Let's fall back on the one thing we all have implanted in us at birth that oh so worrisome conscience. I do not know how many times this has spoiled my fun. How about you, have you ever had the experience of wanting to do something that you saw others doing and they were having what seemed to be a fun time and you wanted to join in? You may say I know right and wrong, but do you? Yes, all our lives we have had an ongoing battle with the aspects of doing right and wrong. Many have come to the point of ignoring the warnings from this source that we no longer pay attention to it, or we choose to alter its original purpose and only hear what makes us feel good. Which is not always what is right. God has a different standard. He says His ways are higher than ours.

2 CHRONICLES 7:10-15 KING JAMES VERSION

[10] And on the three and twentieth day of the seventh month he sent the people away into their tents, glad and merry in heart for the goodness that the Lord had shewed unto David, and to Solomon, and to Israel his people.

[11] Thus Solomon finished the house of the Lord, and the king's house: and all that came into Solomon's heart to make in the house of the Lord, and in his own house, he prosperously effected.

[12] And the Lord appeared to Solomon by night, and said unto him, I have heard thy prayer, and have chosen this place to myself for an house of sacrifice.

[13] If I shut up heaven that there be no rain, or if I command the locusts to devour the land, or if I send pestilence among my people;

[14] If my people, which are called by my name, shall humble themselves, and pray, and seek my face, and turn from their wicked ways; then will I hear from heaven, and will forgive their sin, and will heal their land.

[15] Now mine eyes shall be open, and mine ears attent unto the prayer that is made in this place.

JOB 31:3-10 NEW INTERNATIONAL VERSION

[3] Is it not ruin for the wicked,
   disaster for those who do wrong?
[4] Does he not see my ways
   and count my every step?
[5] "If I have walked with falsehood
   or my foot has hurried after deceit—
[6] let God weigh me in honest scales
   and he will know that I am blameless—
[7] if my steps have turned from the path,
   if my heart has been led by my eyes,
   or if my hands have been defiled,
[8] then may others eat what I have sown,
   and may my crops be uprooted.
[9] "If my heart has been enticed by a woman,

> or if I have lurked at my neighbor's door,
> ¹⁰ then may my wife grind another man's grain,
> and may other men sleep with her.

ISAIAH 55:7-9 KING JAMES VERSION

> ⁷ Let the wicked forsake his way, and the unrighteous man his thoughts: and let him return unto the Lord, and he will have mercy upon him; and to our God, for he will abundantly pardon.
> ⁸ For my thoughts are not your thoughts, neither are your ways my ways, saith the Lord.
> ⁹ For as the heavens are higher than the earth, so are my ways higher than your ways, and my thoughts than your thoughts.

EPHESIANS 2:1-3 KING JAMES VERSION

> ¹ And you hath he quickened, who were dead in trespasses and sins;
> ² Wherein in time past ye walked according to the course of this world, according to the prince of the power of the air, the spirit that now worketh in the children of disobedience:
> ³ Among whom also we all had our conversation in times past in the lusts of our flesh, fulfilling the desires of the flesh and of the mind; and were by nature the children of wrath, even as others.
> Colossians 3:5-7 King James Version
> ⁵ Mortify therefore your members which are upon the earth; fornication, uncleanness, inordinate affection, evil concupiscence, and covetousness, which is idolatry:
> ⁶ For which things' sake the wrath of God cometh on the children of disobedience:
> ⁷ In the which ye also walked some time, when ye lived in them.

Isn't it amazing how many times we quote the old testament and so many say it is to be ignored.

The next thing which we need to understand from these scriptures is that God sees all of us as being part of the disobedient until we truly repent. He leads us to understand that when we are following the desires and thoughts of the flesh that this was motivated by the world and the power which is labeled the evil powers of the air. It is our selfishness which causes so much wrong to be done in this life. The more educated we become the more likely we are to reject that we are inherently sinful. Science and philosophy will not lead us to understand this without the work of the Holy

Spirit. We are more often mislead into believing we are ok if we consider that we are not hurting someone else, it is fine. So, we find here God tells us we without our belief in Him that we are sinners and followers of Satan. We will deny this in the flesh since we do not see ourselves as Satan's followers. No, we do not see ourselves as being that bad. Others who are Satanic cult followers do this not us. No, we are blind to this except when we are led to believe in Jesus as our saviour. Many of us in our natural state do not see Satan, God, or Jesus as real. Many even though they may accept the teachings of Jesus that do not understand many times they are missing the point.

EPHESIANS 4:11-25 EASY-TO-READ VERSION

11 And that same Christ gave these gifts to people: He made some to be apostles, some to be prophets, some to go and tell the Good News, and some to care for and teach God's people.[a]

12 Christ gave these gifts to prepare God's holy people for the work of serving, to make the body of Christ stronger.

13 This work must continue until we are all joined together in what we believe and in what we know about the Son of God. Our goal is to become like a full-grown man—to look just like Christ and have all his perfection.

14 Then we will no longer be like babies. We will not be people who are always changing like a ship that the waves carry one way and then another. We will not be influenced by every new teaching we hear from people who are trying to deceive us—those who make clever plans and use every kind of trick to fool others into following the wrong way.

15 No, we will speak the truth with love. We will grow to be like Christ in every way. He is the head,

16 and the whole body depends on him. All the parts of the body are joined and held together, with each part doing its own work. This causes the whole body to grow and to be stronger in love.

The Way You Should Live

17 I have something from the Lord to tell you. I warn you: Don't continue living like those who don't believe. Their thoughts are worth nothing.

18 They have no understanding, and they know nothing because they refuse to listen. So they cannot have the life that God gives.

19 They have lost their feeling of shame and use their lives to do what is morally wrong. More and more they want to do all kinds of evil.

20 But that way of life is nothing like what you learned when you came to know Christ.
21 I know that you heard about him, and in him you were taught the truth. Yes, the truth is in Jesus.
22 You were taught to leave your old self. This means that you must stop living the evil way you lived before. That old self gets worse and worse, because people are fooled by the evil they want to do. 23 You must be made new in your hearts and in your thinking.
24 Be that new person who was made to be like God, truly good and pleasing to him.
25 So you must stop telling lies. "You must always speak the truth to each other,"[b] because we all belong to each other in the same body.

    Footnotes
    a) *Ephesians 4:11 to care for ... people Literally, "to be shepherds and teachers."*
    b) *Ephesians 4:25 Quote from Zech. 8:16.*

ZECHARIAH 8:16 EASY-TO-READ VERSION

16 But you must do this: Tell the truth to your neighbors. When you make decisions in your cities, be fair and do what is right. Do what brings peace.

EPHESIANS 5:1-20 KING JAMES VERSION

1 Be ye therefore followers of God, as dear children;
2 And walk in love, as Christ also hath loved us, and hath given himself for us an offering and a sacrifice to God for a sweetsmelling savour.
3 But fornication, and all uncleanness, or covetousness, let it not be once named among you, as becometh saints;
4 Neither filthiness, nor foolish talking, nor jesting, which are not convenient: but rather giving of thanks.
5 For this ye know, that no whoremonger, nor unclean person, nor covetous man, who is an idolater, hath any inheritance in the kingdom of Christ and of God.
6 Let no man deceive you with vain words: for because of these things cometh the wrath of God upon the children of disobedience.
7 Be not ye therefore partakers with them.
8 For ye were sometimes darkness, but now are ye light in the Lord: walk as children of light:

⁹ *(For the fruit of the Spirit is in all goodness and righteousness and truth;)*
¹⁰ *Proving what is acceptable unto the Lord.*
¹¹ *And have no fellowship with the unfruitful works of darkness, but rather reprove them.*
¹² *For it is a shame even to speak of those things which are done of them in secret.*
¹³ *But all things that are reproved are made manifest by the light: for whatsoever doth make manifest is light.*
¹⁴ *Wherefore he saith, Awake thou that sleepest, and arise from the dead, and Christ shall give thee light.*
¹⁵ *See then that ye walk circumspectly, not as fools, but as wise,*
¹⁶ *Redeeming the time, because the days are evil.*
¹⁷ *Wherefore be ye not unwise, but understanding what the will of the Lord is.*
¹⁸ *And be not drunk with wine, wherein is excess; but be filled with the Spirit;*
¹⁹ *Speaking to yourselves in psalms and hymns and spiritual songs, singing and making melody in your heart to the Lord;*
²⁰ *Giving thanks always for all things unto God and the Father in the name of our Lord Jesus Christ;*

Here Paul is led to share even more explicitly what is sinful conduct. Note lying is listed as well as fornication covetousness, greed, foolish talk or jesting all uncleanness and the works of darkness which are many. So many things which we strive for in this life are considered sinful behavior. That which is not born out of Godly love is labeled as sinful.

Here we are given an outline of sinful behaviors which we are made to see as sin only through the work of Christ. Now let's turn from this to the good works which we are called to grasp hold of while resisting the urge to return to the sinful behavior or to shun sinful behavior.

Summary

1 JOHN 3:18 KING JAMES VERSION

¹⁸ *My little children, let us not love in word, neither in tongue; but in deed and in truth.*

1 JOHN 3:18 EASY-TO-READ VERSION

18 My children, our love should not be only words and talk. No, our love must be real. We must show our love by the things we do.

So, what is to be gained from the book of Ephesian's prophecy?
1. Christ expects new converts to come repentant and with a willingness to start anew. We are to come as we are with the desire for His conversion work within us. We have the Holy Spirit to work this conversion work in us.

John 3:2-4 King James Version
2 The same came to Jesus by night, and said unto him, Rabbi, we know that thou art a teacher come from God: for no man can do these miracles that thou doest, except God be with him.
3 Jesus answered and said unto him, Verily, verily, I say unto thee, Except a man be born again, he cannot see the kingdom of God.
4 Nicodemus saith unto him, How can a man be born when he is old? can he enter the second time into his mother's womb, and be born?

John 3:6-15 Easy-to-Read Version
6 The only life people get from their human parents is physical. But the new life that the Spirit gives a person is spiritual.
7 Don't be surprised that I told you, 'You must be born again.'
8 The wind blows wherever it wants to. You hear it, but you don't know where it is coming from or where it is going. It is the same with everyone who is born from the Spirit."
9 Nicodemus asked, "How is all this possible?"
10 Jesus said, "You are an important teacher of Israel, and you still don't understand these things?
11 The truth is, we talk about what we know. We tell about what we have seen. But you people don't accept what we tell you.
12 I have told you about things here on earth, but you do not believe me. So I'm sure you will not believe me if I tell you about heavenly things!
13 The only one who has ever gone up to heaven is the one who came down from heaven—the Son of Man.
14 "Moses lifted up the snake in the desert.[a] It is the same with the Son of Man. He must be lifted up too. 15 Then everyone who believes in him can have eternal life."[b]
Footnotes

a. *John 3:14 Moses lifted ... desert* When God's people were dying from snake bites, God told Moses to put a brass snake on a pole for them to look at and be healed. See Num. 21:4-9.
b. *John 3:15* Some scholars think that Jesus' words to Nicodemus continue through verse 21.

1 Peter 1:22-24 Easy-to-Read Version

22 You have made yourselves pure by obeying the truth. Now you can have true love for your brothers and sisters. So love each other deeply—with all your heart.

23 You have been born again. This new life did not come from something that dies. It came from something that cannot die. You were born again through God's life-giving message that lasts forever.

24 The Scriptures say,
"Our lives are like the grass of spring,
  and any glory we enjoy is like the beauty of a wildflower.
The grass dries up and dies,
  and the flower falls to the ground."

2. Our first duty as a Christian is to seek the kingdom of God and His righteousness and allow the Holy Spirit to transform us into His image. He understands our needs. Yes, we must eat and be protected from the elements. Establishing His kingdom should be our number one priority.

Matthew 6:30-34 King James Version

30 Wherefore, if God so clothe the grass of the field, which to day is, and to morrow is cast into the oven, shall he not much more clothe you, O ye of little faith?

31 Therefore take no thought, saying, What shall we eat? or, What shall we drink? or, Wherewithal shall we be clothed?

32 (For after all these things do the Gentiles seek:) for your heavenly Father knoweth that ye have need of all these things.

33 But seek ye first the kingdom of God, and his righteousness; and all these things shall be added unto you.

> *³⁴ Take therefore no thought for the morrow: for the morrow shall take thought for the things of itself. Sufficient unto the day is the evil thereof.*

3. We need to shun our previous lifestyles which were to follow those worldly teachings and the designs of Satan and allow the Holy Spirit to change us so that we desire to be transformed into doing things out of love and compassion.
4. We need to study scripture to learn what is considered the works of darkness.

   > *2 Timothy 2:14-16 Easy-to-Read Version*
   > **A Worker Who Pleases God**
   > *¹⁴ Keep on telling everyone these truths. And warn them before God not to argue about words. Such arguments don't help anyone, and they ruin those who listen to them.*
   > *¹⁵ Do your best to be the kind of person God will accept, and give yourself to him. Be a worker who has no reason to be ashamed of his work, one who applies the true teaching in the right way.*
   > *¹⁶ Stay away from people who talk about useless things that are not from God. That kind of talk will lead a person more and more against God.*

5. We need to take to singing spiritual songs and allow these to resonate in our spirit not the songs of the world which lead us into the wrong way of thinking. As we are told as a man thinks so is he.

   > *Ephesians 5:18-20 Easy-to-Read Version*
   > *¹⁸ Don't be drunk with wine, which will ruin your life, but be filled with the Spirit.*
   > *¹⁹ Encourage each other with psalms, hymns, and spiritual songs. Sing and make music in your hearts to the Lord.*
   > *²⁰ Always give thanks to God the Father for everything in the name of our Lord Jesus Christ.*
   >
   > *Colossians 3:15-17 Easy-to-Read Version*
   > *¹⁵ Let the peace that Christ gives control your thinking. It is for peace that you were chosen to be together in one body.[a] And always be thankful.*
   > *¹⁶ Let the teaching of Christ live inside you richly. Use all wisdom to teach and counsel each other. Sing psalms, hymns, and spiritual songs with thankfulness in your hearts to God.*

¹⁷ Everything you say and everything you do should be done for Jesus your Lord. And in all you do, give thanks to God the Father through Jesus.
Footnotes
    a. Colossians 3:15 body Christ's spiritual body, meaning the church—his people.

6. The acts of sorcery, sexual immorality in any form, idol worship, sacrifices to idols, and living a lifestyle of sin are not acceptable. Idol worship can be defined as anything which we honor more than God. We see greed labeled as idolatry as well as many other things.

> *1 Samuel 15:22-24 Easy-to-Read Version*
> ²² But Samuel answered, "Which pleases the Lord more: burnt offerings and sacrifices or obeying his commands? It is better to obey the Lord than to offer sacrifices to him. It is better to listen to him than to offer the fat from rams.
> ²³ Refusing to obey is as bad as the sin of sorcery. Being stubborn and doing what you want is like the sin of worshiping idols. You refused to obey the Lord's command, so he now refuses to accept you as king."
> ²⁴ Then Saul said to Samuel, "I have sinned. I did not obey the Lord's commands, and I did not do what you told me. I was afraid of the people, and I did what they said.
>
> *Galatians 5:19-21 Easy-to-Read Version*
> ¹⁹ The wrong things the sinful self does are clear: committing sexual sin, being morally bad, doing all kinds of shameful things,
> ²⁰ worshiping false gods, taking part in witchcraft, hating people, causing trouble, being jealous, angry or selfish, causing people to argue and divide into separate groups,
> ²¹ being filled with envy, getting drunk, having wild parties, and doing other things like this. I warn you now as I warned you before: The people who do these things will not have a part in God's kingdom.
>
> *Colossians 3:4-6 King James Version*
> ⁴ When Christ, who is our life, shall appear, then shall ye also appear with him in glory.
> ⁵ Mortify therefore your members which are upon the earth; fornication, uncleanness, inordinate affection, evil concupiscence, and covetousness, which is idolatry:

> *⁶ For which things' sake the wrath of God cometh on the children of disobedience:*

7. We cannot serve two masters. If we continue to cling to our old way of life, we are in peril. These old ways will hinder the work of the Church. This includes following prevailing social norms which have not been instituted by Christ. We are to leave behind the imperfect past.

> *Matthew 6:23-34 Easy-to-Read Version*
> *²³ But if you look at people in a selfish way, you will be full of darkness. And if the only light you have is really darkness, you have the worst kind of darkness.[a]*
> *²⁴ "You cannot serve two masters at the same time. You will hate one and love the other, or you will be loyal to one and not care about the other. You cannot serve God and Money[b] at the same time.*
> *Put God's Kingdom First*
> *²⁵ "So I tell you, don't worry about the things you need to live—what you will eat, drink, or wear. Life is more important than food, and the body is more important than what you put on it. ²⁶ Look at the birds. They don't plant, harvest, or save food in barns, but your heavenly Father feeds them. Don't you know you are worth much more than they are?*
> *²⁷ You cannot add any time to your life by worrying about it.*
> *²⁸ "And why do you worry about clothes? Look at the wildflowers in the field. See how they grow. They don't work or make clothes for themselves.*
> *²⁹ But I tell you that even Solomon, the great and rich king, was not dressed as beautifully as one of these flowers.*
> *³⁰ If God makes what grows in the field so beautiful, what do you think he will do for you? It's just grass—one day it's alive, and the next day someone throws it into a fire. But God cares enough to make it beautiful. Surely he will do much more for you. Your faith is so small!*
> *³¹ "Don't worry and say, 'What will we eat?' or 'What will we drink?' or 'What will we wear?'*
> *³² That's what those people who don't know God are always thinking about. Don't worry, because your Father in heaven knows that you need all these things.*

³³ *What you should want most is God's kingdom and doing what he wants you to do. Then he will give you all these other things you need.*
³⁴ *So don't worry about tomorrow. Each day has enough trouble of its own. Tomorrow will have its own worries.*
   Footnotes
   a. Matthew 6:23 Literally, "22 The lamp of the body is the eye. So, if your eye is pure, your whole body will be full of light. 23 But if your eye is evil, your whole body will be dark. So, if the light in you is darkness, how much is the darkness."
   b. Matthew 6:24 Money Or " mamona," an Aramaic word meaning "wealth."

8. We have to renounce the old sinful self to allow the work of the Holy Spirit to change us.
9. Jesus is willing to work in us if we allow Him to do this. It is the inner self which must be changed into His likeness if we allow this to occur.
10. We must give the Holy Spirit permission to change our spirit to match that of Jesus.
11. We cannot continue in the old way of life with its ideas and be acceptable to Christ. We are to recognize in ourselves the polluted and evil practices of the past if we are to be acceptable to Him.
12. Jesus can provide all that is needed for us to change and will provide a new personality, which is indicated by a new name.
13. We need to teach and learn the aspects of a new life in Christ and what to expect as a result.
14. Many have been baptized unto repentance but have not received the gift of the Holy Spirit which regenerates our inner man. Nor can we have an understanding of eternal life without the Holy Spirit.
15. Tribulation is to be expected in our life as Christians.

Deuteronomy 4:29-31 Amplified Bible
²⁹ *But from there you will seek the Lord your God, and you will find Him if you search for Him with all your heart and all your soul.*

30 When you are in distress and tribulation and all these things come on you, in the latter days you will return to the Lord your God and listen to His voice.
31 For the Lord your God is a merciful and compassionate God; He will not fail you, nor destroy you, nor forget the covenant with your fathers which He swore to them.

John 16:32-33 King James Version

32 Behold, the hour cometh, yea, is now come, that ye shall be scattered, every man to his own, and shall leave me alone: and yet I am not alone, because the Father is with me.

33 These things I have spoken unto you, that in me ye might have peace. In the world ye shall have tribulation: but be of good cheer; I have overcome the world.

John 16:32-33 Amplified Bible

32 Take careful notice: an hour is coming, and has arrived, when you will all be scattered, each to his own home, leaving Me alone; and yet I am not alone, because the Father is with Me.

33 I have told you these things, so that in Me you may have [perfect] peace. In the world you have tribulation and distress and suffering, but be courageous [be confident, be undaunted, be filled with joy]; I have overcome the world." [My conquest is accomplished, My victory abiding.]

There is a difference between doing good works and good deeds. Scripture describes the difference in this way. The things we do to glorify us or to make us feel good or we do to promote our own glory among men are so called good deeds. This we should shy away from. The bible describes good works as those which we do out the love of Christ for our fellow brothers and sister and for the glory of God the Father. Jesus provided the parable of the good Samaritan as an example of this. In this we are allowed to see the way God does things. We see so called religion and social customs at work along with personal concerns and the work of love. Each representation provides the why and how we decide to act in most situations.

LUKE 10:25-37 EASY-TO-READ VERSION

A Story About the Good Samaritan
25 Then an expert in the law stood up to test Jesus. He said, "Teacher, what must I do to get eternal life?"

²⁶ Jesus said to him, "What is written in the law? What do you understand from it?"

²⁷ The man answered, "'Love the Lord your God with all your heart, all your soul, all your strength, and all your mind.'[a] Also, 'Love your neighbor the same as you love yourself.'[b]"

²⁸ Jesus said, "Your answer is right. Do this and you will have eternal life."

²⁹ But the man wanted to show that the way he was living was right. So he said to Jesus, "But who is my neighbor?"

³⁰ To answer this question, Jesus said, "A man was going down the road from Jerusalem to Jericho. Some robbers surrounded him, tore off his clothes, and beat him. Then they left him lying there on the ground almost dead.

³¹ "It happened that a Jewish priest was going down that road. When he saw the man, he did not stop to help him. He walked away.

³² Next, a Levite came near. He saw the hurt man, but he went around him. He would not stop to help him either. He just walked away.

³³ "Then a Samaritan man traveled down that road. He came to the place where the hurt man was lying. He saw the man and felt very sorry for him.

³⁴ The Samaritan went to him and poured olive oil and wine[c] on his wounds. Then he covered the man's wounds with cloth. The Samaritan had a donkey. He put the hurt man on his donkey, and he took him to an inn. There he cared for him.

³⁵ The next day, the Samaritan took out two silver coins and gave them to the man who worked at the inn. He said, 'Take care of this hurt man. If you spend more money on him, I will pay it back to you when I come again.'"

³⁶ Then Jesus said, "Which one of these three men do you think was really a neighbor to the man who was hurt by the robbers?"

³⁷ The teacher of the law answered, "The one who helped him." Jesus said, "Then you go and do the same."

Footnotes
a) Luke 10:27 Quote from Deut. 6:5.
b) Luke 10:27 Quote from Lev. 19:18.
c) Luke 10:34 olive oil and wine These were used like medicine to soften and clean wounds.

> **DEUTERONOMY 6:5 EASY-TO-READ VERSION**
>
> *⁵ You must love the Lord your God with all your heart, with all your soul, and with all your strength.*
>
> **LEVITICUS 19:18 EASY-TO-READ VERSION**
>
> *¹⁸ Forget about the wrong things people do to you. Don't try to get even. Love your neighbor as yourself. I am the Lord.*

Please don't do as the Ephesians did and get caught up in seeing your good works as bringing salvation and not the grace of God through Christ Jesus.

Chapter 6

The Basis of our sin; Our selfish Nature

EPHESIANS 2:1-8 EASY-TO-READ VERSION

From Death to Life
¹ In the past you were spiritually dead because of your sins and the things you did against God.
² Yes, in the past your lives were full of those sins. You lived the way the world lives, following the ruler of the evil powers[a] that are above the earth. That same spirit is now working in those who refuse to obey God.
³ In the past all of us lived like that, trying to please our sinful selves. We did all the things our bodies and minds wanted. Like everyone else in the world, we deserved to suffer God's anger just because of the way we were.
⁴ But God is rich in mercy, and he loved us very much.
⁵ We were spiritually dead because of all we had done against him. But he gave us new life together with Christ. (You have been saved by God's grace.)
⁶ Yes, it is because we are a part of Christ Jesus that God raised us from death and seated us together with him in the heavenly places.
⁷ God did this so that his kindness to us who belong to Christ Jesus would clearly show for all time to come the amazing richness of his grace.
⁸ I mean that you have been saved by grace because you believed. You did not save yourselves; it was a gift from God.
    Footnotes

a) *Ephesians 2:2 ruler of the evil powers See "Satan" in the Word List*

REVELATION 2:18-29 KING JAMES VERSION (KJV)

18 And unto the angel of the Church in Thyatira write; These things saith the Son of God, who hath his eyes like unto a flame of fire, and his feet are like fine brass;
19 I know thy works, and charity, and service, and faith, and thy patience, and thy works; and the last to be more than the first.
20 Notwithstanding I have a few things against thee, because thou sufferest that woman Jezebel, which calleth herself a prophetess, to teach and to seduce my servants to commit fornication, and to eat things sacrificed unto idols.
21 And I gave her space to repent of her fornication; and she repented not.
22 Behold, I will cast her into a bed, and them that commit adultery with her into great tribulation, except they repent of their deeds.
23 And I will kill her children with death; and all the Churches shall know that I am he which searcheth the reins and hearts: and I will give unto every one of you according to your works.
24 But unto you I say, and unto the rest in Thyatira, as many as have not this doctrine, and which have not known the depths of Satan, as they speak; I will put upon you none other burden.
25 But that which ye have already hold fast till I come.
26 And he that overcometh, and keepeth my works unto the end, to him will I give power over the nations:
27 And he shall rule them with a rod of iron; as the vessels of a potter shall they be broken to shivers: even as I received of my Father.
28 And I will give him the morning star.
29 He that hath an ear, let him hear what the Spirit saith unto the Churches.

Most of us are blind or ignorant of the factors which motivate us and what we strive for in this life. I know for me until I was taught by the Holy Spirit I was ignorant to a lot of this. Most of my life was spent going to church and to school and observing the world around me. I choose those things which appealed to me and which I tried to grasp. I wanted nice clothes, a nice home, a nice family, and to run around and be like the men around me. I was learning to take what I could to grow my wealth and position. I thought if I did not cause too much harm, I was ok. I was blind to the fact that these factors were not what God wanted. Yes, I had memorized the ten commandments but the true meaning and understanding of these illuded me. I felt if I lied a little and did not do anything outrageous that I was ok. I wanted to fit into the American dream. Yet there was something which kept telling me more was needed. Even after I was baptized at 29 years old I did not realize the need for inner change in my life. I saw others seeking wealth and prosperity. I wanted this for myself. I wanted nice clothes, a nice car, and a big house. Succes in my job was a big part of life and church came next. It wasn't until I learned that being a follower of Christ was more than following a slate of moral conduct that I began to understand where I was being led astray. Yes, I was into performance based Christianity and not the transforming work of the Holy Spirit. I felt as if I could have the best of both worlds, comfort and being a disciple of Christ. I now know there is a world of difference between the two. There is a way that seems good to men and a way which is right. I was following the way which seemed good.

PROVERBS 16:24-26 AMPLIFIED BIBLE

²⁴ Pleasant words are like a honeycomb,
Sweet and delightful to the soul and healing to the body.
²⁵ There is a way which seems right to a man and appears straight before him,
But its end is the way of death.
²⁶ The appetite of a worker works for him,
For his hunger urges him on.

Social standards and social norms were the prize for me and I had no true understanding of eternal life and what truly surrendering to Christ was. So, I am being led to help you avoid some of the same pitfalls in your journey with Christ. We must come to know all things which can cause us to be misled and what are our true motivations in life. They were there in scripture all along, but I kept seeing my conduct and that of others as true religion. But now I understand there are factors which we take for granted which are leading us down the wrong path. So, examine these things more carefully. In Ephesians I find that the Lord is telling us things which are not obvious to us. In the previous chapter these were touched on lightly so let us go into this scripture a little deeper to gain wisdom.

Our following of worldly teachings is pointed out in the book of Ephesians. So, what are these? I know from the ten commandments I am not to lust after stuff which my neighbor has.

EXODUS 20:17 AMPLIFIED BIBLE

17 "You shall not covet [that is, selfishly desire and attempt to acquire] your neighbor's house; you shall not covet your neighbor's wife, or his male servant, or his female servant, or his ox, or his donkey, or anything that belongs to your neighbor."

PSALM 81:11-13 KING JAMES VERSION

11 But my people would not hearken to my voice; and Israel would none of me.
12 So I gave them up unto their own hearts' lust: and they walked in their own counsels.
13 Oh that my people had hearkened unto me, and Israel had walked in my ways!

1 JOHN 2:15-17 KING JAMES VERSION

15 Love not the world, neither the things that are in the world. If any man love the world, the love of the Father is not in him.

16 For all that is in the world, the lust of the flesh, and the lust of the eyes, and the pride of life, is not of the Father, but is of the world.

17 And the world passeth away, and the lust thereof: but he that doeth the will of God abideth for ever.

1 JOHN 2:15-17 AMPLIFIED BIBLE

Do Not Love the World
15 Do not love the world [of sin that opposes God and His precepts], nor the things that are in the world. If anyone loves the world, the love of the Father is not in him.
16 For all that is in the world—the lust and sensual craving of the flesh and the lust and longing of the eyes and the boastful pride of life [pretentious confidence in one's resources or in the stability of earthly things]—these do not come from the Father, but are from the world.

¹⁷ *The world is passing away, and with it its lusts [the shameful pursuits and ungodly longings]; but the one who does the will of God and carries out His purposes lives forever.*

It is so plain now. I have been following the ways of the world. Can you remember the saying about "having two chickens in the pot" or "keeping up with the Jones." How are these sayings encouraging us and how have they influenced our lives?

During the depression people strove to have enough to eat. In this day and time, we strive to have gourmet meals. It is not just to satisfy our need for food but to work to have the most we can afford. Pamper yourself is the message today. Enjoy the best of everything based on your ability to do so. Strive to have more to get more. It was keeping up with the Jones. Well, it is not now enough to keep up with them, but it is to surpass them.

So, we want higher pay, greater positions, be our own boss, and make as much as you can get before you leave this life. Fulfilling our bucket list is now our ultimate goal. Our goal is now for us to do everything our heart desires in this life since we only have one life to live. We strive to get more to have more. We want more prestige and more recognition. We want to be recognized for who we are, it is more important to have the right title than to do a good job. So many job titles have been changed not because the roles have changed but to bring more prestige to the position. We all are encouraged to seek to be your own boss, control your own destiny. Wealth is power and money is power, get rich, live the life of leisure is now the goal. We are being taught more and more that God wants us to be rich and that we deserve the riches of the world. The way of the world is all about me, my, and mine. If it enhances my lifestyle, then do it. If it causes me to be noticed, then do it. If it makes me feel good, do it. If you can, do not leave this life without experiencing all the good things it has to offer. We are becoming more and more conditioned to turn inward for pleasure not for examination but self-gratification.

I am led to point out that in the beginning God told Adam to care for the earth and he was given power to name all animals. We have been tricked into understanding that when we are told we are to have dominion over the earth that means we can do what we want with it. That is not the case. We have been fooled by the ways of the world into thinking it is ours to do with as we want. We can reject this teaching and choose to follow God's way which calls us to provide for the benefit of all, but we have chosen to follow the path of self-gratification rather than the path of oneness. We can resist the devil and his ways but because they coincide so closely with our selfishness we accept these readily. Yes, we have the divine and the devilish struggling with each of us. Consider this from scripture.

> **1 CORINTHIANS 13:2-13 KING JAMES VERSION (KJV)**
> *² And though I have the gift of prophecy, and understand all mysteries, and all knowledge; and though I have all faith, so that I could remove mountains, and have not charity, I am nothing.*
> *³ And though I bestow all my goods to feed the poor, and though I give my body to be burned, and have not charity, it profiteth me nothing.*
> *⁴ Charity suffereth long, and is kind; charity envieth not; charity vaunteth not itself, is not puffed up,*
> *⁵ Doth not behave itself unseemly, seeketh not her own, is not easily provoked, thinketh no evil;*
> *⁶ Rejoiceth not in iniquity, but rejoiceth in the truth;*
> *⁷ Beareth all things, believeth all things, hopeth all things, endureth all things.*
> *⁸ Charity never faileth: but whether there be prophecies, they shall fail; whether there be tongues, they shall cease; whether there be knowledge, it shall vanish away.*
> *⁹ For we know in part, and we prophesy in part.*
> *¹⁰ But when that which is perfect is come, then that which is in part shall be done away.*
> *¹¹ When I was a child, I spake as a child, I understood as a child, I thought as a child: but when I became a man, I put away childish things.*
> *¹² For now we see through a glass, darkly; but then face to face: now I know in part; but then shall I know even as also I am known.*
> *¹³ And now abideth faith, hope, charity, these three; but the greatest of these is charity.*

We are more than flesh and blood. There is a spirit within which is the true source of who we are, and which is in control of what we do. God wants to remove the bondage of the world's teachings and those of Satan. The Lord wants to free us to be one with Him and with each other. No man, woman, or child is to be considered any better or greater than any other by the Lord and it should be the same with us. Jesus tells we are all to be equal in Him.

EPHESIANS 4:1-10 KING JAMES VERSION

4 I therefore, the prisoner of the Lord, beseech you that ye walk worthy of the vocation wherewith ye are called,
2 With all lowliness and meekness, with longsuffering, forbearing one another in love;
3 Endeavouring to keep the unity of the Spirit in the bond of peace.
4 There is one body, and one Spirit, even as ye are called in one hope of your calling;
5 One Lord, one faith, one baptism,
6 One God and Father of all, who is above all, and through all, and in you all.
7 But unto every one of us is given grace according to the measure of the gift of Christ.
8 Wherefore he saith, When he ascended up on high, he led captivity captive, and gave gifts unto men.
9 (Now that he ascended, what is it but that he also descended first into the lower parts of the earth?
10 He that descended is the same also that ascended up far above all heavens, that he might fill all things.)

GALATIANS 3:27-29 KING JAMES VERSION

27 For as many of you as have been baptized into Christ have put on Christ.
28 There is neither Jew nor Greek, there is neither bond nor free, there is neither male nor female: for ye are all one in Christ Jesus.
29 And if ye be Christ's, then are ye Abraham's seed, and heirs according to the promise.

COLOSSIANS 3:10-12 KING JAMES VERSION

10 And have put on the new man, which is renewed in knowledge after the image of him that created him:
11 Where there is neither Greek nor Jew, circumcision nor uncircumcision, Barbarian, Scythian, bond nor free: but Christ is all, and in all.
12 Put on therefore, as the elect of God, holy and beloved, bowels of mercies, kindness, humbleness of mind, meekness, longsuffering;

He can say so much in a word and how it is used. That is what is lacking in the walk of the everyday Christian today. Many have been lulled into inactivity by the sermons which they hear that draws them to place their lustful desires above the pure love of God and of our fellow man. Therefore, the word "service" today is mute in the church. We don't get it. We have not seen the need for it. When we do many things will change. To us, service is just attending church and doing something nice for those less fortunate than us. To many we now have many who say they believe in Christ but no longer attend church or claim affiliation with any religion. **_No!_** This is not what Jesus wants or what we need. Not many offer themselves in complete surrender to Him and His work in them. Here is the difference in the church at Pentecost in scripture and the reality of the church today. It is our lack of service which is most outstanding. We do a lot of what man considers good things, but these, without service (doing things in the spirit of perfect love the love of and for the glory of God), mean nothing. Service is the actual ability to worship Him in spirit and truth, which is expected in all who are called by His name. We have demeaned the term service and identified it as our duty to attend Church or our duty to be a nice person. That is why scripture says we are to be constantly drawn out in prayer. That is, we are to be in constant unison with God the Father and His Son and with each other. All that we do to honor and praise God is a prayer to Him.

ROMANS 12:1-3 KING JAMES VERSION (KJV)

¹ I beseech you therefore, brethren, by the mercies of God, that ye present your bodies a living sacrifice, holy, acceptable unto God, which is your reasonable service.
² And be not conformed to this world: but be ye transformed by the renewing of your mind, that ye may prove what is that good, and acceptable, and perfect, will of God.
³ For I say, through the grace given unto me, to every man that is among you, not to think of himself more highly than he ought to think; but to think soberly, according as God hath dealt to every man the measure of faith.

TITUS 2:11-15 KING JAMES VERSION (KJV)

¹¹ For the grace of God that bringeth salvation hath appeared to all men,

¹² Teaching us that, denying ungodliness and worldly lusts, we should live soberly, righteously, and godly, in this present world;

¹³ Looking for that blessed hope, and the glorious appearing of the great God and our Saviour Jesus Christ;

¹⁴ Who gave himself for us, that he might redeem us from all iniquity, and purify unto himself a peculiar people, zealous of good works.

¹⁵ These things speak, and exhort, and rebuke with all authority. Let no man despise thee.

ACTS 8:1-25 KING JAMES VERSION (KJV)

⁸ And Saul was consenting unto his death. And at that time there was a great persecution against the Church which was at Jerusalem; and they were all scattered abroad throughout the regions of Judaea and Samaria, except the apostles.

² And devout men carried Stephen to his burial, and made great lamentation over him.

³ As for Saul, he made havock of the Church, entering into every house, and haling men and women committed them to prison.

⁴ Therefore they that were scattered abroad went every where preaching the word.

⁵ Then Philip went down to the city of Samaria, and preached Christ unto them.

⁶ And the people with one accord gave heed unto those things which Philip spake, hearing and seeing the miracles which he did.

⁷ For unclean spirits, crying with loud voice, came out of many that were possessed with them: and many taken with palsies, and that were lame, were healed.

⁸ And there was great joy in that city.

⁹ But there was a certain man, called Simon, which beforetime in the same city used sorcery, and bewitched the people of Samaria, giving out that himself was some great one:

¹⁰ To whom they all gave heed, from the least to the greatest, saying, This man is the great power of God.

¹¹ And to him they had regard, because that of long time he had bewitched them with sorceries.

12 But when they believed Philip preaching the things concerning the kingdom of God, and the name of Jesus Christ, they were baptized, both men and women.
13 Then Simon himself believed also: and when he was baptized, he continued with Philip, and wondered, beholding the miracles and signs which were done.
14 Now when the apostles which were at Jerusalem heard that Samaria had received the word of God, they sent unto them Peter and John:
15 Who, when they were come down, prayed for them, that they might receive the Holy Ghost:
16 (For as yet he was fallen upon none of them: only they were baptized in the name of the Lord Jesus.)
17 Then laid they their hands on them, and they received the Holy Ghost.
18 And when Simon saw that through laying on of the apostles' hands the Holy Ghost was given, he offered them money,
19 Saying, Give me also this power, that on whomsoever I lay hands, he may receive the Holy Ghost.
20 But Peter said unto him, Thy money perish with thee, because thou hast thought that the gift of God may be purchased with money.
21 Thou hast neither part nor lot in this matter: for thy heart is not right in the sight of God.
22 Repent therefore of this thy wickedness, and pray God, if perhaps the thought of thine heart may be forgiven thee.
23 For I perceive that thou art in the gall of bitterness, and in the bond of iniquity.
24 Then answered Simon, and said, Pray ye to the Lord for me, that none of these things which ye have spoken come upon me.
25 And they, when they had testified and preached the word of the Lord, returned to Jerusalem, and preached the gospel in many villages of the Samaritans.

Sorcerers and magicians demonstrate acts that get our attention and because of the feats which they can perform, many place them on a pedestal. Yes, there are powers at work we cannot explain or duplicate because the source for them resides in an evil power and his followers. We do not want to admit this is real, but it is. Today we identify this as superstition rather than reality because we are guided by what we call the principles of science and our intelligence rather than accept the fact of a real devil and a real God (a spiritual existence beyond our sight). Our perceptions are based on our physical senses and if we can't touch, see, or taste, the experience or can't prove it by scientific examination or our interpretation of physical evidence for it, we don't accept it. We are provided evidence of these in scripture by the magicians in Pharaoh's court and Balaam and the sorcerers that Paul and others faced. These are stated repeatedly in scripture, but we dismiss these as fables or fairy tales or allegory. We are enthralled by modern day magicians, most of whom perform feats which are just tricks or illusions, but there are true magicians who receive power from Satan. There are sorcerers in this day and time at work who can receive power from Satan. Today we might call them mediums or spiritual advisors. We try dismissing this as trickery. Some of it is but, some of it is not. We will see a resurgence of this in the anti-Christ and some of His predecessors. It is Satan using a counterfeit of the power of the Spirit, which is expressed as healing, speaking in tongues, prophecy and more. He can impart special abilities to His followers just as God does, but those of God carry His power which can overcome those of the devil. We will have to grasp the concept that there is a spiritual dimension not just the physical one bound by time and space as we know it. Einstein was on the verge of proving the eternal or spiritual realm with his theory of relativity. Einstein's theory indicates that nothing is ever destroyed, it just changes form or state. Einstein was allowed to express eternal life in scientific terms. Consider this scripture. Refer to my first book Formulas in Scripture $E = MC^2$ for further information on this formula in spiritual terms.

EPHESIANS 3:10-12 AMPLIFIED BIBLE

[10] So now through the church the multifaceted wisdom of God [in all its countless aspects] might now be made known [revealing the mystery] to the [angelic] rulers and authorities in the heavenly places.
[11] This is in accordance with [the terms of] the eternal purpose which He carried out in Christ Jesus our Lord,
[12] in whom we have boldness and confident access through faith in Him [that is, our faith gives us sufficient courage to freely and openly approach God through Christ].

EXODUS 7:9-12 KING JAMES VERSION (KJV)

9 When Pharaoh shall speak unto you, saying, Shew a miracle for you: then thou shalt say unto Aaron, Take thy rod, and cast it before Pharaoh, and it shall become a serpent.
10 And Moses and Aaron went in unto Pharaoh, and they did so as the Lord had commanded: and Aaron cast down his rod before Pharaoh, and before his servants, and it became a serpent.
11 Then Pharaoh also called the wise men and the sorcerers: now the magicians of Egypt, they also did in like manner with their enchantments.
12 For they cast down every man his rod, and they became serpents: but Aaron's rod swallowed up their rods.

ACTS 13:5-7 KING JAMES VERSION (KJV)

5 And when they were at Salamis, they preached the word of God in the synagogues of the Jews: and they had also John to their minister.
6 And when they had gone through the isle unto Paphos, they found a certain sorcerer, a false prophet, a Jew, whose name was Barjesus:
7 Which was with the deputy of the country, Sergius Paulus, a prudent man; who called for Barnabas and Saul, and desired to hear the word of God.

Of course, many today are taught not to believe the exodus in Genesis actually occurred so they are unwilling to accept this reference. Nor do they want to accept that God prophesied the restoration of the nation of Israel. Yet we keep looking for the battle of Armageddon and the rapture. Pray that the Lord will confirm the existence of the two realms to you and if you approach Him in faith you will receive the answer. It is more than the good feeling we have when we say we can feel the good Spirit, or we are in His presence. I have experienced both realms and I tell you that heaven is best. I have seen both God and the devil. God is the best choice. The devil has a black appearance which is so dark that light cannot penetrate him. Yet some accept him as an angel of light. God is the source of light and truth. Please excuse my wandering but in my spirit, I feel this must be said.

Summary

We must come to understand that there is a difference between how we live, and the way God is calling us to live. Our way of life is not what he wants for us. There is a difference between reading and quoting scripture and living the life God is calling us to live in this world. Israel missed the mark. So, should we do the same? That is why the Lord stated that we should "be in the world and not of it." We can do this by learning to do what pleases God.

MATTHEW 18:6-8 AMPLIFIED BIBLE

⁶ but whoever causes one of these little ones who believe in Me to stumble and sin [by leading him away from My teaching], it would be better for him to have a heavy millstone [as large as one turned by a donkey] hung around his neck and to be drowned in the depth of the sea.
Stumbling Blocks
⁷ "Woe (judgment is coming) to the world because of stumbling blocks and temptations to sin! It is inevitable that stumbling blocks come; but woe to the person on whose account or through whom the stumbling block comes!
⁸ "If your hand or your foot causes you to stumble and sin, cut it off and throw it away from you [that is, remove yourself from the source of temptation]; it is better for you to enter life crippled or lame, than to have two hands or two feet and be thrown into everlasting fire.

MARK 4:18-20 AMPLIFIED BIBLE

¹⁸ And others are the ones on whom seed was sown among the thorns; these are the ones who have heard the word,
¹⁹ but the worries and cares of the world [the distractions of this age with its worldly pleasures], and the deceitfulness [and the false security or glamour] of wealth [or fame], and the passionate desires for all the other things creep in and choke out the word, and it becomes unfruitful.
²⁰ And those [in the last group] are the ones on whom seed was sown on the good soil; and they hear the word [of God, the good news regarding the way of salvation] and accept it and bear fruit—thirty, sixty, and a hundred times as much [as was sown]."

JOHN 12:45-47 AMPLIFIED BIBLE

⁴⁵ *And whoever sees Me sees the One who sent Me.*
⁴⁶ *I have come as Light into the world, so that everyone who believes and trusts in Me [as Savior—all those who anchor their hope in Me and rely on the truth of My message] will not continue to live in darkness.*
⁴⁷ *If anyone hears My words and does not keep them, I do not judge him; for I did not come to judge and condemn the world [that is, to initiate the final judgment of the world], but to save the world.*

EPHESIANS 5:1-10 EASY-TO-READ VERSION

¹ *You are God's dear children, so try to be like him.*
² *Live a life of love. Love others just as Christ loved us. He gave himself for us—a sweet-smelling offering and sacrifice to God.*
³ *But there must be no sexual sin among you. There must not be any kind of evil or selfishly wanting more and more, because such things are not right for God's holy people.*
⁴ *Also, there must be no evil talk among you. Don't say things that are foolish or filthy. These are not for you. But you should be giving thanks to God.*
⁵ *You can be sure of this: No one will have a place in the kingdom of Christ and of God if that person commits sexual sins, or does evil things, or is a person who selfishly wants more and more. A greedy person like that is serving a false god.*
⁶ *Don't let anyone fool you with words that are not true. God gets very angry when people who don't obey him talk like that.*
⁷ *So don't have anything to do with them.*
⁸ *In the past you were full of darkness, but now you are full of light in the Lord. So live like children who belong to the light.*
⁹ *This light produces every kind of goodness, right living, and truth.* ¹⁰ *Try to learn what pleases the Lord.*

We need to understand that Godly values are different from those we have learned in this world. We only do good because of the Love which He implants within us. We need to relearn to follow the direction of the conscience which was originally placed in us and the direction of the Holy Spirit rather than the values and goals the world leads us to follow which are directly influenced by Satan. God expresses that we are selfish but He wants this selfishness to be replaced with a loving and compassionate nature. We have lessons we have all learned in life which differ so far from what God created us to be and do. He states we were created to perform good works, not to do a phony copy of this.

ISAIAH 57:11-13 EASY-TO-READ VERSION

11 You did not remember me.
  You did not even notice me!
So who were you worrying about?
  Who were you afraid of?
  Why did you lie?
Look, I have been quiet for a long time.
  Is that why you didn't honor me?
12 I could tell about your 'good works' and all the 'religious' things you do, but that will not help you.
13 When you need help, you cry to those false gods that you have gathered around you.
  Let them help you!
But I tell you, the wind will blow them all away. A puff of wind will blow them all away. But the one who depends on me will get the land I promised and enjoy my holy mountain.[a]"
  Footnotes
    a. *Isaiah 57:13 holy mountain Mount Zion, one of the mountains Jerusalem was built on.*

Yes, we have all heard it is better to give than receive but is that truly our motive in giving? Is it that we just want to feed our ego and see ourselves as being good and not bad. It is difficult to convince someone that he or she is following the wrong pattern in their life. That is why so many people follow what makes them feel good and not what is genuinely good. We need to learn there is a difference. Our walk with God requires that we understand the difference and not be fooled into reverting back to our old self-serving motives after we have once repented and started on a new path, one of discipleship. Yes, being a disciple or student, no not just a student but one who truly lives the lifestyle of Jesus. One where we choose to do only those things we see the Father and Son do. We establish this by following the Holy Spirit and learning from the mistakes or sins of those who have gone before us as portrayed in scripture. We also learn those things from these sources what is pleasing to God. In our history courses we need to learn the lessons of the past. If we do the same things others before us had done, we will get the same result. Crime racism, slavery, immoral acts and so many other sins will persist as long as we duplicate the acts of the past. Look to the future which God calls us to develop.

We need the support of each other so we can come to the point where no one is unimportant or is valueless. God desires that none should perish and so should we. We need to learn that if we continue to follow the teachings of man and his ways this will lead to death. We all will physically die someday, but spiritual death is something we should learn is where we are headed when we choose to follow the world and the evil one rather than the plan of salvation God has outlined.

It is the inner person that needs to change not our outward appearance. Do not be fooled by what seems good but delight in the truth. I know I for a long time I was aspired to live the good life as man defined it. Now I know the difference and am working in partnership with the Holy Spirit to become more like Jesus so that what I do may be please Father God and not men. I want to love Him and Jesus and the Holy Spirit and you all with the same love with which God loves His creation.

EPHESIANS 2:1-8 EASY-TO-READ VERSION

From Death to Life

[1] *In the past you were spiritually dead because of your sins and the things you did against God.*

[2] *Yes, in the past your lives were full of those sins. You lived the way the world lives, following the ruler of the evil powers[a] that are above the earth. That same spirit is now working in those who refuse to obey God.*

[3] *In the past all of us lived like that, trying to please our sinful selves. We did all the things our bodies and minds wanted. Like everyone else in the world, we deserved to suffer God's anger just because of the way we were.*

[4] *But God is rich in mercy, and he loved us very much.*

[5] *We were spiritually dead because of all we had done against him. But he gave us new life together with Christ. (You have been saved by God's grace.)*

[6] *Yes, it is because we are a part of Christ Jesus that God raised us from death and seated us together with him in the heavenly places.*

7 God did this so that his kindness to us who belong to Christ Jesus would clearly show for all time to come the amazing richness of his grace.
8 I mean that you have been saved by grace because you believed. You did not save yourselves; it was a gift from God.
  Footnotes
  a) Ephesians 2:2 ruler of the evil powers See "Satan" in the Word List

I want the transforming grace which God instituted long before time began to be implanted in my Spirit so that when Jesus returns, I will know Him because I will be like Him. This is because I am learning to follow the guidance which He has provided. I am learning what pleases God. Like Paul I am not yet perfect but that is what I am striving to achieve, the high calling of Christ Jesus.

EPHESIANS 4:17-32 AMPLIFIED BIBLE

The Christian's Walk
17 So this I say, and solemnly affirm together with the Lord [as in His presence], that you must no longer live as the [unbelieving] Gentiles live, in the futility of their minds [and in the foolishness and emptiness of their souls],
18 for their [moral] understanding is darkened and their reasoning is clouded; [they are] alienated and self-banished from the life of God [with no share in it; this is] because of the [willful] ignorance and spiritual blindness that is [deep-seated] within them, because of the hardness and insensitivity of their heart.
19 And they, [the ungodly in their spiritual apathy], having become callous and unfeeling, have given themselves over [as prey] to unbridled sensuality, eagerly craving the practice of every kind of impurity [that their desires may demand].
20 But you did not learn Christ in this way!
21 If in fact you have [really] heard Him and have been taught by Him, just as truth is in Jesus [revealed in His life and personified in Him],
22 that, regarding your previous way of life, you put off your old self [completely discard your former nature], which is being corrupted through deceitful desires,
23 and be continually renewed in the spirit of your mind [having a fresh, untarnished mental and spiritual attitude],
24 and put on the new self [the regenerated and renewed nature], created in God's image, [godlike] in the righteousness and

holiness of the truth [living in a way that expresses to God your gratitude for your salvation].
²⁵ Therefore, rejecting all falsehood [whether lying, defrauding, telling half-truths, spreading rumors, any such as these], speak truth each one with his neighbor, for we are all parts of one another [and we are all parts of the body of Christ].
²⁶ Be angry [at sin—at immorality, at injustice, at ungodly behavior], yet do not sin; do not let your anger [cause you shame, nor allow it to] last until the sun goes down.
²⁷ And do not give the devil an opportunity [to lead you into sin by holding a grudge, or nurturing anger, or harboring resentment, or cultivating bitterness].
²⁸ The thief [who has become a believer] must no longer steal, but instead he must work hard [making an honest living], producing that which is good with his own hands, so that he will have something to share with those in need.
²⁹ Do not let unwholesome [foul, profane, worthless, vulgar] words ever come out of your mouth, but only such speech as is good for building up others, according to the need and the occasion, so that it will be a blessing to those who hear [you speak].
³⁰ And do not grieve the Holy Spirit of God [but seek to please Him], by whom you were sealed and marked [branded as God's own] for the day of redemption [the final deliverance from the consequences of sin].
³¹ Let all bitterness and wrath and anger and clamor [perpetual animosity, resentment, strife, fault-finding] and slander be put away from you, along with every kind of malice [all spitefulness, verbal abuse, malevolence].
³² Be kind and helpful to one another, tender-hearted [compassionate, understanding], forgiving one another [readily and freely], just as God in Christ also forgave [a]you.
Footnotes
a)   Ephesians 4:32 Two early mss read us.

EPHESIANS 5:1-20 AMPLIFIED BIBLE

Be Imitators of God
¹ Therefore become imitators of God [copy Him and follow His example], as well-beloved children [imitate their father];
² and walk continually in love [that is, value one another— practice empathy and compassion, unselfishly seeking the best for others], just as Christ also loved you and gave Himself up for us,

an offering and sacrifice to God [slain for you, so that it became] a sweet fragrance.

³ But sexual immorality and all [moral] impurity [indecent, offensive behavior] or greed must not even be hinted at among you, as is proper among saints [for as believers our way of life, whether in public or in private, reflects the validity of our faith].

⁴ Let there be no filthiness and silly talk, or coarse [obscene or vulgar] joking, because such things are not appropriate [for believers]; but instead speak of your thankfulness [to God].

⁵ For be sure of this: no immoral, impure, or greedy person—for that one is [in effect] an idolater—has any inheritance in the kingdom of Christ and God [for such a person places a higher value on something other than God].

⁶ Let no one deceive you with empty arguments [that encourage you to sin], for because of these things the wrath of God comes upon the sons of disobedience [those who habitually sin].

⁷ So do not participate or even associate with them [in the rebelliousness of sin].

⁸ For once you were darkness, but now you are light in the Lord; walk as children of Light [live as those who are native-born to the Light]

⁹ (for the fruit [the effect, the result] of the Light consists in all goodness and righteousness and truth),

¹⁰ trying to learn [by experience] what is pleasing to the Lord [and letting your lifestyles be examples of what is most acceptable to Him—your behavior expressing gratitude to God for your salvation].

¹¹ Do not participate in the worthless and unproductive deeds of darkness, but instead expose them [by exemplifying personal integrity, moral courage, and godly character]; 12 for it is disgraceful even to mention the things that such people practice in secret.

¹³ But all things become visible when they are exposed by the light [of God's precepts], for [a]it is light that makes everything visible.

¹⁴ For this reason He says,

"Awake, sleeper,

And arise from the dead,

And Christ will shine [as dawn] upon you and give you light."

¹⁵ Therefore see that you walk carefully [living life with honor, purpose, and courage; shunning those who tolerate and enable evil], not as the unwise, but as wise [sensible, intelligent, discerning people],

¹⁶ [b]making the very most of your time [on earth, recognizing and taking advantage of each opportunity and using it with wisdom and diligence], because the days are [filled with] evil.

¹⁷ Therefore do not be foolish and thoughtless, but understand and firmly grasp what the will of the Lord is.

¹⁸ Do not get drunk with wine, for that is wickedness (corruption, stupidity), but be filled with the [Holy] Spirit and constantly guided by Him.

¹⁹ [c]Speak to one another in psalms and hymns and spiritual songs, [offering praise by] singing and making melody with your heart to the Lord;

²⁰ always giving thanks to God the Father for all things, in the name of our Lord Jesus Christ;

Footnotes

a) Ephesians 5:13 Paul, who was privileged to study under the brilliant Gamaliel (Acts 22:3), is probably speaking from the viewpoint of ancient Greek science. Even the philosopher Plato maintained that vision essentially is the process of light forming an image of an object it touches and conveying that image to the eyes. So Paul may mean that what is actually seen is an image composed of light (like the photographic process), and since light is always reliable and its physical properties are constant, nothing exposed to light escapes being revealed. Spiritually speaking, to the extent that a believer functions as Light (v 8), he will expose the sins of unbelievers simply by his presence, just as it is the nature of light to expose whatever it touches.

b) Ephesians 5:16 The Greek word in this verse means "buy up at the market place." Opportunity is regarded as a commodity to be used by believers.

c) Ephesians 5:19 The Greeks had a tradition of holding drinking parties (called, in the singular, a symposium) where the object was to sing the praises of the pagan gods while becoming drunk. Perhaps with this tradition in mind, Paul instructs believers to "be filled" instead with the Holy Spirit and to sing meaningful praises to God.

CHAPTER 7

Paul Explains Our Defensive Tools To Resist Sinful Influences

EPHESIANS 3 KING JAMES VERSION

¹For this cause I Paul, the prisoner of Jesus Christ for you Gentiles,
² If ye have heard of the dispensation of the grace of God which is given me to you-ward:
³ How that by revelation he made known unto me the mystery; (as I wrote afore in few words,
⁴ Whereby, when ye read, ye may understand my knowledge in the mystery of Christ)
⁵ Which in other ages was not made known unto the sons of men, as it is now revealed unto his holy apostles and prophets by the Spirit;
⁶ That the Gentiles should be fellowheirs, and of the same body, and partakers of his promise in Christ by the gospel:
⁷ Whereof I was made a minister, according to the gift of the grace of God given unto me by the effectual working of his power.
⁸ Unto me, who am less than the least of all saints, is this grace given, that I should preach among the Gentiles the unsearchable riches of Christ;
⁹ And to make all men see what is the fellowship of the mystery, which from the beginning of the world hath been hid in God, who created all things by Jesus Christ:
¹⁰ To the intent that now unto the principalities and powers in heavenly places might be known by the church the manifold wisdom of God,
¹¹ According to the eternal purpose which he purposed in Christ Jesus our Lord:

12 *In whom we have boldness and access with confidence by the faith of him.*
13 *Wherefore I desire that ye faint not at my tribulations for you, which is your glory.*
14 *For this cause I bow my knees unto the Father of our Lord Jesus Christ,*
15 *Of whom the whole family in heaven and earth is named,*
16 *That he would grant you, according to the riches of his glory, to be strengthened with might by his Spirit in the inner man;*
17 *That Christ may dwell in your hearts by faith; that ye, being rooted and grounded in love,*
18 *May be able to comprehend with all saints what is the breadth, and length, and depth, and height;*
19 *And to know the love of Christ, which passeth knowledge, that ye might be filled with all the fulness of God.*
20 *Now unto him that is able to do exceeding abundantly above all that we ask or think, according to the power that worketh in us,*
21 *Unto him be glory in the church by Christ Jesus throughout all ages, world without end. Amen.*

EPHESIANS 5:1-20 AMPLIFIED BIBLE

Be Imitators of God
1 *Therefore become imitators of God [copy Him and follow His example], as well-beloved children [imitate their father];*
2 *and walk continually in love [that is, value one another—practice empathy and compassion, unselfishly seeking the best for others], just as Christ also loved you and gave Himself up for us, an offering and sacrifice to God [slain for you, so that it became] a sweet fragrance.*
3 *But sexual immorality and all [moral] impurity [indecent, offensive behavior] or greed must not even be hinted at among you, as is proper among saints [for as believers our way of life, whether in public or in private, reflects the validity of our faith].*
4 *Let there be no filthiness and silly talk, or coarse [obscene or vulgar] joking, because such things are not appropriate [for believers]; but instead speak of your thankfulness [to God].*
5 *For be sure of this: no immoral, impure, or greedy person—for that one is [in effect] an idolater—has any inheritance in the kingdom of Christ and God [for such a person places a higher value on something other than God].*

⁶ Let no one deceive you with empty arguments [that encourage you to sin], for because of these things the wrath of God comes upon the sons of disobedience [those who habitually sin].
⁷ So do not participate or even associate with them [in the rebelliousness of sin].
⁸ For once you were darkness, but now you are light in the Lord; walk as children of Light [live as those who are native-born to the Light]
⁹ (for the fruit [the effect, the result] of the Light consists in all goodness and righteousness and truth),
¹⁰ trying to learn [by experience] what is pleasing to the Lord [and letting your lifestyles be examples of what is most acceptable to Him—your behavior expressing gratitude to God for your salvation].
¹¹ Do not participate in the worthless and unproductive deeds of darkness, but instead expose them [by exemplifying personal integrity, moral courage, and godly character]; 12 for it is disgraceful even to mention the things that such people practice in secret.
¹³ But all things become visible when they are exposed by the light [of God's precepts], for [a]it is light that makes everything visible.
¹⁴ For this reason He says,
"Awake, sleeper,
And arise from the dead,
And Christ will shine [as dawn] upon you and give you light."
¹⁵ Therefore see that you walk carefully [living life with honor, purpose, and courage; shunning those who tolerate and enable evil], not as the unwise, but as wise [sensible, intelligent, discerning people],
¹⁶ [b]making the very most of your time [on earth, recognizing and taking advantage of each opportunity and using it with wisdom and diligence], because the days are [filled with] evil.
¹⁷ Therefore do not be foolish and thoughtless, but understand and firmly grasp what the will of the Lord is.
¹⁸ Do not get drunk with wine, for that is wickedness (corruption, stupidity), but be filled with the [Holy] Spirit and constantly guided by Him.
¹⁹ [c]Speak to one another in psalms and hymns and spiritual songs, [offering praise by] singing and making melody with your heart to the Lord;
²⁰ always giving thanks to God the Father for all things, in the name of our Lord Jesus Christ;

Footnotes

a) *Ephesians 5:13 Paul, who was privileged to study under the brilliant Gamaliel (Acts 22:3), is probably speaking from the viewpoint of ancient Greek science. Even the philosopher Plato maintained that vision essentially is the process of light forming an image of an object it touches and conveying that image to the eyes. So Paul may mean that what is actually seen is an image composed of light (like the photographic process), and since light is always reliable and its physical properties are constant, nothing exposed to light escapes being revealed. Spiritually speaking, to the extent that a believer functions as Light (v 8), he will expose the sins of unbelievers simply by his presence, just as it is the nature of light to expose whatever it touches.*

b) *Ephesians 5:16 The Greek word in this verse means "buy up at the market place." Opportunity is regarded as a commodity to be used by believers.*

c) *Ephesians 5:19 The Greeks had a tradition of holding drinking parties (called, in the singular, a symposium) where the object was to sing the praises of the pagan gods while becoming drunk. Perhaps with this tradition in mind, Paul instructs believers to "be filled" instead with the Holy Spirit and to sing meaningful praises to God.*

EPHESIANS 6:10-18 AMPLIFIED BIBLE

The Armor of God

[10] In conclusion, be strong in the Lord [draw your strength from Him and be empowered through your union with Him] and in the power of His [boundless] might.

[11] Put on the full armor of God [for His precepts are like the splendid armor of a heavily-armed soldier], so that you may be able to [successfully] stand up against all the schemes and the strategies and the deceits of the devil.

[12] For our struggle is not against flesh and blood [contending only with physical opponents], but against the rulers, against the powers, against the world forces of this [present] darkness, against the spiritual forces of wickedness in the heavenly (supernatural) places.

[13] Therefore, put on the complete armor of God, so that you will be able to [successfully] resist and stand your ground in the evil day [of danger], and having done everything [that the crisis

demands], to stand firm [in your place, fully prepared, immovable, victorious]. ¹⁴ So stand firm and hold your ground, having [a]tightened the wide band of truth (personal integrity, moral courage) around your waist and having put on the breastplate of righteousness (an upright heart),

¹⁵ and having [b]strapped on your feet the gospel of peace in preparation [to face the enemy with firm-footed stability and the readiness produced by the good news].

¹⁶ Above all, lift up the [protective] [c]shield of faith with which you can extinguish all the flaming arrows of the evil one.

¹⁷ And take the helmet of salvation, and the sword of the Spirit, which is the Word of God.

¹⁸ With all prayer and petition pray [with specific requests] at all times [on every occasion and in every season] in the Spirit, and with this in view, stay alert with all perseverance and petition [interceding in prayer] for all [d]God's people.

Footnotes

a) Ephesians 6:14 Lit girded your loins, a phrase often found in the Bible, is an urgent call to get ready for immediate action or a coming event. The phrase is related to the type of clothing worn in ancient times. Before any vigorous activity the loose ends of clothing (tunics, cloaks, mantles, etc.) had to be gathered up and tucked into the wide band worn around the midsection of the body. The band (usually about six inches wide) also served as a kind of pocket or pouch to carry personal items such as a dagger, money or other necessary things. Gird up your mind or gird up your heart are examples of variants of this phrase and call for mental or spiritual preparation for a coming challenge.

b) Ephesians 6:15 A reference to the Roman soldiers' shoes which were studded with hobnails to give them stability on the battlefield.

c) Ephesians 6:16 Here the Greek word refers to the large Roman soldiers' shield designed to protect the entire body. It had an iron frame and was covered in several layers of leather. When soaked in water before a battle the shield could put out the fiery missiles thrown at them by the enemy.

d) Ephesians 6:18 Lit the saints.

Paul is led to describe the battle fronts which we face. These are the flesh or our physical existence, our reasoning processes and finally our spiritual makeup. The way we live our lives is determined by the choices we make and the why and how those choices come about. So, we need to understand the why and how we do what we do. God knows how to give us full control of each of these so that Jesus through the Holy Spirit can make us whole. Whole is defined as being the condition of perfection needed to reside in God's presence. So, we see that Paul addresses these battle fronts in Ephesians and each of the letters to the churches as he is led by the Lord to increase our understanding. Paul informs us how each of these result in different yet final outcomes. See in scripture how he addresses the attributes which are indicative of the way we live. It is the way we act out our inner processes which determines how we play out our daily routines of life. Scripture identifies these attributes and how to control them. Now understand that it is not me who is doing this, but I am doing this as I am led by the Spirit to do so. So, when I say I am doing this it is the Lord who is directing what is being placed in this book. Look again at the entire book Ephesians. Paul is led to address man's need to defend against the forces which result in who we choose to follow. We either follow the worldly design which is controlled by Satan and his corrupted way of reasoning which results in us following sinful conduct and thinking. When we truly choose Jesus as our savior, we give Him permission to correct the corruption which has been embedded in us so that we can learn to live in accordance with God's ordained manners of conduct. Let us investigate some of this guidance we have been provided.

PROVERBS 23:6-8 KING JAMES VERSION

⁶ Eat thou not the bread of him that hath an evil eye, neither desire thou his dainty meats:
⁷ For as he thinketh in his heart, so is he: Eat and drink, saith he to thee; but his heart is not with thee.
⁸ The morsel which thou hast eaten shalt thou vomit up, and lose thy sweet words.

PROVERBS 23:6-8 AMPLIFIED BIBLE

⁶ Do not eat the bread of a selfish man,
Or desire his delicacies;

⁷ *For as he thinks in his heart, so is he [in behavior—one who manipulates].*
He says to you, "Eat and drink,"
Yet his heart is not with you [but it is begrudging the cost].
⁸ *The morsel which you have eaten you will vomit up,*
And you will waste your compliments.

JAMES 1:14-15 KING JAMES VERSION

¹⁴ *But every man is tempted, when he is drawn away of his own lust, and enticed.*
¹⁵ *Then when lust hath conceived, it bringeth forth sin: and sin, when it is finished, bringeth forth death.*

JAMES 1:14-15 AMPLIFIED BIBLE

¹⁴ *But each one is tempted when he is dragged away, enticed and baited [to commit sin] by his own [worldly] desire (lust, passion).*
¹⁵ *Then when the illicit desire has conceived, it gives birth to sin; and when sin has run its course, it gives birth to death.*

LUKE 21:33-35 AMPLIFIED BIBLE

³³ *Heaven and earth will pass away, but My words will not pass away.*
³⁴ *"But be on guard, so that your hearts are not weighed down and depressed with the giddiness of debauchery and the nausea of self-indulgence and the worldly worries of life, and then that day [when the Messiah returns] will not come on you suddenly like a trap;*
³⁵ *for it will come upon all those who live on the face of all the earth.*

SECTION 76:4A-4F DOCTRINE & COVENANTS

[Sec 76:4a] *Thus saith the Lord, concerning all those who know my power, and have been made partakers thereof, and suffered themselves, through the power of the Devil, to be overcome, and to deny the truth, and defy my power;*
[Sec 76:4b] *they are they who are the sons of perdition, of whom I say it had been better for them never to have been born;*
[Sec 76:4c] *for they are vessels of wrath, doomed to suffer the wrath of God, with the Devil and his angels, in eternity, concerning whom I have said there is no forgiveness in this world nor in*
the world to come;

> *[Sec 76:4d] having denied the Holy Spirit, after having received it, and having denied the only begotten Son of the Father; having crucified him unto themselves, and put him to an open shame:*
> *[Sec 76:4e] these are they who shall go away into the lake of fire and brimstone, with the Devil and his angels, and the only ones on whom the second death shall have any power; yea, verily, the only ones who shall not be redeemed in the due time of the Lord, after the sufferings of his wrath;*
> *[Sec 76:4f] for all the rest shall be brought forth by the resurrection of the dead, through the triumph and the glory of the Lamb, who was slain, who was in the bosom of the Father before the worlds were made.*

Paul is led to identify a soldier's armor as our defense against the works of the world produced by Satan and his evil desires. Paul is using common devices to instruct and to help us understand we are under attack. When Paul describes this, we should remember he is describing a defensive device, not something which we use to fight with but one we use for protection. So many today feel that because Paul uses this description that it is up to us to fight for the Lord's way in this world. No that is not what he is saying here. We are told again and again our battle is not with flesh and blood but spiritual wickedness in high places. See in this text we are provided instruction for our spiritual battle and the battle for our mind. Jesus told us it is not what goes into a person's belly which defiles him but that which comes from within.

MATTHEW 15:16-18 AMPLIFIED BIBLE

> [16] *And He said, "Are you still so dull [and unable to put things together]?*
> [17] *Do you not understand that whatever goes into the mouth passes into the stomach, and is eliminated?*
> [18] *But whatever [word] comes out of the mouth comes from the heart, and this is what defiles and dishonors the man.*

So, we are being provided instruction to help the inner man because the inner man is the source of his outward actions which are fleshly works as described in scripture. Review what is provided in scripture.

> **MARK 7:21-23 KING JAMES VERSION**
>
> ²¹ For from within, out of the heart of men, proceed evil thoughts, adulteries, fornications, murders,
> ²² Thefts, covetousness, wickedness, deceit, lasciviousness, an evil eye, blasphemy, pride, foolishness:
> ²³ All these evil things come from within, and defile the man.
>
> **EPHESIANS 6:10-18 KING JAMES VERSION**
>
> ¹⁰ Finally, my brethren, be strong in the Lord, and in the power of his might.
> ¹¹ Put on the whole armour of God, that ye may be able to stand against the wiles of the devil.
> ¹² For we wrestle not against flesh and blood, but against principalities, against powers, against the rulers of the darkness of this world, against spiritual wickedness in high places.
> ¹³ Wherefore take unto you the whole armour of God, that ye may be able to withstand in the evil day, and having done all, to stand.
> ¹⁴ Stand therefore, having your loins girt about with truth, and having on the breastplate of righteousness;
> ¹⁵ And your feet shod with the preparation of the gospel of peace;
> ¹⁶ Above all, taking the shield of faith, wherewith ye shall be able to quench all the fiery darts of the wicked.
> ¹⁷ And take the helmet of salvation, and the sword of the Spirit, which is the word of God:
> ¹⁸ Praying always with all prayer and supplication in the Spirit, and watching thereunto with all perseverance and supplication for all saints;

Look at the way Paul is led to make this description. He starts with the fact we can depend on the Lord and His power. We need to understand there is no power greater than God's, so we need not fear. So many fear the devil and they should not because he is not stronger than us. The devil knows our weaknesses. The devil has learned to use these to entice us to sin because he knows God will punish sinners who do not repent. We can resist the temptations he uses to cloud our judgment. The Holy Spirit in us makes the devil's efforts fruitless. Paul encourages us to be strong in the Lord. Which means for us to believe in the Lord above all else.

Paul is then led to describe the part of our defense using the belt which is related to our being sustained by the truth. Truth comes as the we are led by the Holy Spirit. It is the job of the Holy Spirit to lead us to know all truth. We need to know that God has chosen us and provides salvation to all who repent and accept His offer to provide eternal life and reject eternal death. The devil wants us to join him in eternal death but with God that is not what we have ahead of us. The devil tries over and over to remind us of the sins of our past and that we must be punished for them. The truth is Jesus has accepted the punishment for our sin and we are no longer held in judgement from God for them. Yet the devil keeps trying to work around this and continually keeps sending signals and approaches to attract us back to sinful conduct. The devil did this with Israel when he sent prostitutes to corrupt them and had them to start worshiping false gods. We need to understand when we know the truth it will set us free and we be able to stand firm in our commitment to the Lord. The truth helps to cleanse us by the work of the Holy Spirit when we follow his guidance. Then our nature will be converted by Lord from worldly to holy and righteous.

Next is something so many today ignore. We are told the shoes represent being shod with preparation of the gospel of peace. We hear so much today about fighting physically to protect our rights. Yet the gospel of peace is that we are to identify wrongs perpetrated in the world against man and God's entire creation. This identification includes using the word of the Lord to change these to the Lord's ways rather the way man has instituted wrong treatment and behaviors. The ways of the world have led to pain and suffering for all of God's creation the earth and fullness thereof including mankind. We are to seek peace not only for the earth but with each other. Paul was led to point this out in so many ways. We are told in scripture to seek peace yet the cry in our day in time is to fight for right and fight against those whom we see as our enemies. Teachings today encourage us to fight physically yet that is not the teaching of the Lord. He says if a man strike you turn the other cheek. Yet today so many are arming themselves to the teeth to fight against evil when the Lord says we should defend ourselves against evil. So where is our peace? It is from the Lord and in the way we live and respond to the Holy Spirit. True love is true peace. True love is willing to live a life dedicated to God's ways not to man's ways.

Then Paul is led to include another one of our defenses which is the shield of faith. We must understand we do not always understand or know that God is at work purifying and correcting the misdeeds of men. So, it is by faith we are saved, and it is by faith we are to accept that we have been granted His forgiveness and that we have the gift of eternal life.

> **EPHESIANS 2:7-9 KING JAMES VERSION**
>
> *⁷ That in the ages to come he might shew the exceeding riches of his grace in his kindness toward us through Christ Jesus.*
> *⁸ For by grace are ye saved through faith; and that not of yourselves: it is the gift of God:*
> *⁹ Not of works, lest any man should boast.*

Sometimes it is faith which is all we have because we have not yet received the assurance of these. As scripture puts it faith is the assurance of all things hoped for. In this lies our ability to reason and trust the words of the Lord are true and will not return to Him void or without fulfilment. We do not always see the physical implementation of His promises when we want but that does not mean the promises are not true. So, faith plays a vital role in the life of a Christian. Case in point as a Christian it was more than forty years of my being a Christian before I recognized occasion where God was at work in my life or before I saw angels in real life or experienced some direct communication with the Lord. It was only in the last few months when He discussed with me things which are to occur soon in my life. I have experienced His healing power in so many ways and times. I just confirm He does hold true to His promises.

Paul points to the fiery darts of the wicked. Look in Revelation where Jesus tells a group of believers warning them of persecution by Jews who were not true jews and to expect that some of them would be killed for the sake of the gospel. Others in the first three chapters are told of false prophets and leaders who claimed to be apostles, corrupt doctrines, and leaders teaching things inconsistent with His works. So, you see we have a defense against these influences and so many other ways we are attacked by those followers of Satan who want to cause us to go off course from the true path of Christ.

Then he addresses the helmet of salvation. We don't have physical proofs of this but with the Holy Spirit we can have proofs of this. This is a battle for our mind which is about the way we reason and make our choices. So again, this is the defense we are provided. We have so many fronts from which we are being attacked. We have so many who have been drawn away by claims from scientist who claim religion and gods are just things made up by humans to provide them comfort. Not all scientists do this just as not every preacher who claims to be so is a true representative of the Lord. It is amazing how many have been duped into accepting false teachings and propagating these concepts rather than the true gospel. Paul is inspired to instruct us to continue in prayers for all the saints.

Now we come to the part of the armor which most identify as our call to be on the offense, the sword. Many interpret this as a weapon used to inflict harm on someone else. No that is not what Paul is being led to guide us toward. I was recently listening to one of female evangelist who pointed out that she had taken karate lessons for many years and was almost a black belt which is the highest level of achievement which one can receive in this training. She wanted everyone to know that unlike what most understand, this is not just used to inflict harm. She wanted to draw our attention to the fact that this form of battle had two uses. One is for defense the other is for offense. So here we have the aspect of a sword. It can used offensively or defensively but most of us believe it is a training used to either kill or wound an opponent.

HEBREWS 4:11-13 KING JAMES VERSION

11 Let us labour therefore to enter into that rest, lest any man fall after the same example of unbelief.

12 For the word of God is quick, and powerful, and sharper than any twoedged sword, piercing even to the dividing asunder of soul and spirit, and of the joints and marrow, and is a discerner of the thoughts and intents of the heart.

13 Neither is there any creature that is not manifest in his sight: but all things are naked and opened unto the eyes of him with whom we have to do.

HEBREWS 4:11-13 AMPLIFIED BIBLE

11 Let us therefore make every effort to enter that rest [of God, to know and experience it for ourselves], so that no one will fall by following the same example of disobedience [as those who died in the wilderness].

> ¹² *For the word of God is living and active and full of power [making it operative, energizing, and effective]. It is sharper than any two-edged [a]sword, penetrating as far as the division of the [b]soul and spirit [the completeness of a person], and of both joints and marrow [the deepest parts of our nature], exposing and judging the very thoughts and intentions of the heart.*
> ¹³ *And not a creature exists that is concealed from His sight, but all things are open and exposed, and revealed to the eyes of Him with whom we have to give account.*
> Footnotes
> > a. Hebrews 4:12 In addition to "sword," the word in Greek was used for the knife used by the priests to slit the throats of the sacrificial lambs and for the knife (scalpel) used by a surgeon.
> > b. Hebrews 4:12 "soul and spirit" used here to emphasize the whole person, not two separate entities as in other passages.

Notice I am using the word opponent rather than enemy. Paul is led by the Spirit to have us to understand that or defense lies in the way we interpret the word of God. So, this implies the word of God is of use in the reasoning and spiritual influence for us which directly relates to how we live our lives and the way our inward processes work. Again, it is from within sinful conduct starts and is initiated.

> **MATTHEW 15:11-20 AMPLIFIED BIBLE**
>
> ¹¹ *It is not what goes into the mouth of a man that defiles and dishonors him, but what comes out of the mouth, this defiles and dishonors him."*
> ¹² *Then the disciples came and said to Jesus, "Do You know that the Pharisees were offended when they heard you say this?"*
> ¹³ *He answered, "Every plant which My heavenly Father did not plant will be torn up by the roots.*
> ¹⁴ *Leave them alone; they are blind guides [a][leading blind followers]. If a blind man leads a blind man, both will fall into a pit."*
> The Heart of Man
> ¹⁵ *Peter asked Him, "Explain this parable [about what defiles a person] to us."*
> ¹⁶ *And He said, "Are you still so dull [and unable to put things together]?*

17 *Do you not understand that whatever goes into the mouth passes into the stomach, and is eliminated?*
18 *But whatever [word] comes out of the mouth comes from the heart, and this is what defiles and dishonors the man.*
19 *For out of the heart come evil thoughts and plans, murders, adulteries, sexual immoralities, thefts, false testimonies, slanders (verbal abuse, irreverent speech, blaspheming).*
20 *These are the things which defile and dishonor the man; but eating with [ceremonially] unwashed hands does not defile the man."*

By following what we find in the word of God we learn what pleases and displeases God. We learn to identify sinful conduct and what is righteous conduct. We learn God's promises and about His love and personality and His plan for all humanity.

1 THESSALONIANS 4:1-3 AMPLIFIED BIBLE

Sanctification and Love
1 *Finally, believers, we ask and admonish you in the Lord Jesus, that you follow the instruction that you received from us about how you ought to walk and please God (just as you are actually doing) and that you excel even more and more [pursuing a life of purpose and living in a way that expresses gratitude to God for your salvation].*
2 *For you know what commandments and precepts we gave you by the authority of the Lord Jesus.*
3 *For this is the will of God, that you be sanctified [separated and set apart from sin]: that you abstain and back away from sexual immorality;*

EPHESIANS 4:29-31 AMPLIFIED BIBLE

29 *Do not let unwholesome [foul, profane, worthless, vulgar] words ever come out of your mouth, but only such speech as is good for building up others, according to the need and the occasion, so that it will be a blessing to those who hear [you speak].*
30 *And do not grieve the Holy Spirit of God [but seek to please Him], by whom you were sealed and marked [branded as God's own] for the day of redemption [the final deliverance from the consequences of sin].*
31 *Let all bitterness and wrath and anger and clamor [perpetual animosity, resentment, strife, fault-finding] and slander be put*

away from you, along with every kind of malice [all spitefulness, verbal abuse, malevolence].

He then ends in telling us to be alert with all perseverance using the ways God has provided for our defense.

We can change our outward expression of love. The way we treat each other is very important. So, Paul is led to share in 1st Corinthians to express how loving someone is shown in the way we treat each other. The words he is led to share are treat each other with kindness, and gentleness. We are not to do things out of our selfish desires or motives. We are to be patient with each other. Neither should we be jealous, nor boastful, nor arrogant or irritable nor resentful. We need to learn to enjoy doing what is right and not wrong. We are to believe all things which God says and let the hope of eternal life and forgiveness of sin be yours always. See it here written in scripture.

1 CORINTHIANS 13 KING JAMES VERSION

[1] Though I speak with the tongues of men and of angels, and have not charity, I am become as sounding brass, or a tinkling cymbal.
[2] And though I have the gift of prophecy, and understand all mysteries, and all knowledge; and though I have all faith, so that I could remove mountains, and have not charity, I am nothing.
[3] And though I bestow all my goods to feed the poor, and though I give my body to be burned, and have not charity, it profiteth me nothing.
[4] Charity suffereth long, and is kind; charity envieth not; charity vaunteth not itself, is not puffed up,
[5] Doth not behave itself unseemly, seeketh not her own, is not easily provoked, thinketh no evil;
[6] Rejoiceth not in iniquity, but rejoiceth in the truth;
[7] Beareth all things, believeth all things, hopeth all things, endureth all things.
[8] Charity never faileth: but whether there be prophecies, they shall fail; whether there be tongues, they shall cease; whether there be knowledge, it shall vanish away.
[9] For we know in part, and we prophesy in part.
[10] But when that which is perfect is come, then that which is in part shall be done away.

> **11** When I was a child, I spake as a child, I understood as a child, I thought as a child: but when I became a man, I put away childish things.
> **12** For now we see through a glass, darkly; but then face to face: now I know in part; but then shall I know even as also I am known.
> **13** And now abideth faith, hope, charity, these three; but the greatest of these is charity.

EPHESIANS 4:31-32 AMPLIFIED BIBLE

> **31** Let all bitterness and wrath and anger and clamor [perpetual animosity, resentment, strife, fault-finding] and slander be put away from you, along with every kind of malice [all spitefulness, verbal abuse, malevolence].
> **32** Be kind and helpful to one another, tender-hearted [compassionate, understanding], forgiving one another [readily and freely], just as God in Christ also forgave [a]you.

One other defense which many seem to neglect is the meeting together and using scripture to bolster us up or to build us up. Paul is led to tell us to meet often and to speak words from the Psalms and sing spiritual songs. It is in repeating these we learn. Many of us know words from songs will stick with us longer than things we read. He likens this with being filled with the Spirit. Many do not understand the need for gathering together and the strength it brings to the body. So many give in to the tactic of the devil which appeals to our selfish nature. It is not just me or you but all of us together which is the goal; one body not many; one spirit not many; one God; one baptism.

EPHESIANS 5:18-20 KING JAMES VERSION

> **18** And be not drunk with wine, wherein is excess; but be filled with the Spirit;
> **19** Speaking to yourselves in psalms and hymns and spiritual songs, singing and making melody in your heart to the Lord;
> **20** Giving thanks always for all things unto God and the Father in the name of our Lord Jesus Christ;

EPHESIANS 5:18-20 EASY-TO-READ VERSION

> **18** Don't be drunk with wine, which will ruin your life, but be filled with the Spirit.

[19] *Encourage each other with psalms, hymns, and spiritual songs. Sing and make music in your hearts to the Lord. 20 Always give thanks to God the Father for everything in the name of our Lord Jesus Christ.*

Summary

We have tools available which we can use to shape the environment in which we live. First remember we have the power and might of the Lord and the Holy Spirit. Loving one another is the vital link and reason we are being taught to choose to use the tools which God has provided.

We have the ability to resist the temptation to follow the ways of the world which have been influenced by Satan. Then we have the work of the inbuilt set of right and wrong provided by God, our conscience. We have scriptures and the support of our fellow brothers and sisters in Christ and the promises and guidance contained in the scriptures which help us to know God's will and distinguish God's will from the works of the devil and those of his followers. The devil and his followers try to trick us as the serpent did Eve in the garden. Another is allowing the Lord to provide judgement for the wrongs which have been brought against us. This is difficult but the Lord tells us vengeance is His. By resisting the devil, we are choosing to walk in loving conduct toward everyone and everything.

DEUTERONOMY 32:42-44 KING JAMES VERSION

[42] I will make mine arrows drunk with blood, and my sword shall devour flesh; and that with the blood of the slain and of the captives, from the beginning of revenges upon the enemy.
[43] Rejoice, O ye nations, with his people: for he will avenge the blood of his servants, and will render vengeance to his adversaries, and will be merciful unto his land, and to his people.
[44] And Moses came and spake all the words of this song in the ears of the people, he, and Hoshea the son of Nun.

ROMANS 12:18-20 KING JAMES VERSION

[18] If it be possible, as much as lieth in you, live peaceably with all men.

¹⁹ Dearly beloved, avenge not yourselves, but rather give place unto wrath: for it is written, Vengeance is mine; I will repay, saith the Lord.
²⁰ Therefore if thine enemy hunger, feed him; if he thirst, give him drink: for in so doing thou shalt heap coals of fire on his head.

ISAIAH 59:10-18 AMPLIFIED BIBLE

¹⁰ We grope for a wall like the blind,
We grope like those who have no eyes.
We stumble at midday as in the twilight;
Among those who are healthy we are like dead men.
¹¹ We all groan and growl like bears,
And coo sadly like doves;
We hope for justice, but there is none,
For salvation, but it is far from us.
¹² For our transgressions are multiplied before You [O Lord],
And our sins testify against us;
For our transgressions are with us,
And we know and recognize our wickedness [our sin, our injustice, our wrongdoing]:
¹³ Rebelling against and denying the Lord,
Turning away from [following] our God,
Speaking oppression and revolt,
Conceiving and muttering from the heart lying words.
¹⁴ Justice is pushed back,
And righteous behavior stands far away;
For truth has fallen in the city square,
And [a]integrity cannot enter.
¹⁵ Yes, truth is missing;
And he who turns away from evil makes himself a prey.
Now the Lord saw it,
And it [b]displeased Him that there was no justice.
¹⁶ He saw that there was no man,
And was amazed that there was no one to intercede [on behalf of truth and right];
Therefore His own arm brought salvation to Him,
And His own righteousness sustained Him.
¹⁷ For He [the Lord] put on righteousness like a coat of armor,
And salvation like a helmet on His head;
He put on garments of vengeance for clothing
And covered Himself with zeal [and great love for His people] as a cloak.

**¹⁸ As their deeds deserve, so He will repay:
Wrath to His adversaries, retribution to His enemies;
To the islands and coastlands He will repay.
   Footnotes
      a.   Isaiah 59:14 Lit straightforwardness.
      b.   Isaiah 59:15 Lit was evil in His eyes.**

I can remember the days when the Green Bay Packers were the best team on the field for years. The theme then was the best offense is the best defense. Now the tide has changed, and it seems like it is only the best offense which wins. Looks can be deceptive because without a defense no team can win. We are living in an age where many feel that they must retake our country by force for God. So many do not understand force is not how God will rule the earth. It is through His loving nature and compassion that the battle between good and evil will win. Yes, we all have heard about the last battle. But the Lord has let us know that He is and always will have the final say in all matters. We all have a part in this work it is not to fight with flesh but with the good fight of faith. Look, stop, and listen to what the Lord has to say to the churches. Preach and practice the gospel of peace and let the Lord fight our battles. Let our lifestyles do the preaching not just words. The words are for teaching. The Lord has already won. All creation will celebrate the final victory. Jesus said it on the cross: "it is finished." The end is in sight and has been foretold. When are we going to accept our task is to live a life under the direction and guidance of the Lord. No man takes this honor unto himself. Again, we are to make the choice to love rather than follow the fleshly lusts which we once allowed to control what we did and why we did it.

We need to understand fleshly lusts come from within and are used to satisfy our feelings emotions and all our senses. Answer the question can I be angry and not sin? Or can I do things which only make me feel self-satisfied.

MATTHEW 5:21-23 AMPLIFIED BIBLE

Personal Relationships
²¹ "You have heard that it was said to the men of old, 'You shall not murder,' and 'Whoever murders shall be [a]guilty before the court.'

[22] But I say to you that everyone who continues to be angry with his brother or harbors malice against him shall be guilty before the court; and whoever speaks [contemptuously and insultingly] to his brother, [b]'Raca (You empty-headed idiot)!' shall be guilty before the supreme court (Sanhedrin); and whoever says, 'You fool!' shall be in danger of the [c]fiery hell.

[23] So if you are presenting your offering at the altar, and while there you remember that your brother has something [such as a grievance or legitimate complaint] against you,

Footnotes

a. Matthew 5:21 Or liable to.
b. Matthew 5:22 A severe Aramaic insult.
c. Matthew 5:22 Gr Gehenna, a Greek version of the Hebrew for Valley of Hinnom, a ravine where garbage was burned continuously, located just south of Jerusalem. Often regarded in ancient times as symbolic of hell (the lake of fire), a realm reserved for the wicked. Mentioned in Matt 5:22, 29, 30; 10:28; 18:9; 23:15, 33; Mark 9:43, 45, 47; Luke 12:5; James 3:6.

The Lord states He will replace the sinful conduct of man with His righteousness. When this happens, all we do is an expression of Godly love which The Lord has implanted in our heart, mind, and spirit. We can then be able to truly live out the following scripture.

1 CORINTHIANS 13:1-8 KING JAMES VERSION

[1] Though I speak with the tongues of men and of angels, and have not charity, I am become as sounding brass, or a tinkling cymbal.

[2] And though I have the gift of prophecy, and understand all mysteries, and all knowledge; and though I have all faith, so that I could remove mountains, and have not charity, I am nothing.

[3] And though I bestow all my goods to feed the poor, and though I give my body to be burned, and have not charity, it profiteth me nothing.

[4] Charity suffereth long, and is kind; charity envieth not; charity vaunteth not itself, is not puffed up,

[5] Doth not behave itself unseemly, seeketh not her own, is not easily provoked, thinketh no evil;

[6] Rejoiceth not in iniquity, but rejoiceth in the truth;

[7] Beareth all things, believeth all things, hopeth all things, endureth all things.

⁸ *Charity never faileth: but whether there be prophecies, they shall fail; whether there be tongues, they shall cease; whether there be knowledge, it shall vanish away.*

LUKE 6:34-36 KING JAMES VERSION

³⁴ *And if ye lend to them of whom ye hope to receive, what thank have ye? for sinners also lend to sinners, to receive as much again.*
³⁵ *But love ye your enemies, and do good, and lend, hoping for nothing again; and your reward shall be great, and ye shall be the children of the Highest: for he is kind unto the unthankful and to the evil.*
³⁶ *Be ye therefore merciful, as your Father also is merciful.*

EPHESIANS 5:18-20 KING JAMES VERSION

¹⁸ *And be not drunk with wine, wherein is excess; but be filled with the Spirit;*
¹⁹ *Speaking to yourselves in psalms and hymns and spiritual songs, singing and making melody in your heart to the Lord;*
²⁰ *Giving thanks always for all things unto God and the Father in the name of our Lord Jesus Christ;*

EPHESIANS 5:18-20 EASY-TO-READ VERSION

¹⁸ *Don't be drunk with wine, which will ruin your life, but be filled with the Spirit.*
¹⁹ *Encourage each other with psalms, hymns, and spiritual songs. Sing and make music in your hearts to the Lord.*
²⁰ *Always give thanks to God the Father for everything in the name of our Lord Jesus Christ.*

Our role is just to obey and submit to Him and follow His direction and then all these things will be added unto us. The mandate is "seek ye first the kingdom of God." This entails relearning and reestablishing the new life we are called to establish. We do this by living a righteous life. Not by force nor by power but by my Spirit says the Lord. This is the first step in becoming a true disciple of Christ.

MATTHEW 6:30-34 AMPLIFIED BIBLE

³⁰ *But if God so clothes the grass of the field, which is alive and green today and tomorrow is [cut and] thrown [as fuel] into the furnace, will He not much more clothe you? You of little faith!*

31 Therefore do not worry or be anxious (perpetually uneasy, distracted), saying, 'What are we going to eat?' or 'What are we going to drink?' or 'What are we going to wear?'
32 For the [pagan] Gentiles eagerly seek all these things; [but do not worry,] for your heavenly Father knows that you need them.
33 But first and most importantly seek (aim at, strive after) His kingdom and His righteousness [His way of doing and being right—the attitude and character of God], and all these things will be given to you also.
34 "So do not worry about tomorrow; for tomorrow will worry about itself. Each day has enough trouble of its own.

We can make all the laws we want and enforce them with our power but only He can change the heart of mankind so that He may be glorified that we might be made to be with Him being perfected through the work of Christ Jesus. He calls us to live a righteous life and not be enforcers of the law. The true law is one which is embedded in us, Godly love.

1 PETER 1:21-23 KING JAMES VERSION

21 Who by him do believe in God, that raised him up from the dead, and gave him glory; that your faith and hope might be in God.
22 Seeing ye have purified your souls in obeying the truth through the Spirit unto unfeigned love of the brethren, see that ye love one another with a pure heart fervently:
23 Being born again, not of corruptible seed, but of incorruptible, by the word of God, which liveth and abideth for ever.

That is His work. He instituted a set of laws for the Israelites which none were able to follow. Neither are we, so why should we be so pious by promoting laws which none can follow? The moral code we trust is unworthy of the Lord. We just need to submit to the Lord's will and allow Him to do the work of changing our character. We are to be led by the Holy Spirit and allow the Lord's work to be lived out here on earth as it is in heaven. It is by following The Lord's guidance we come into the kingdom which is ruled by the pure love of God. Look back at Enoch and see what he did or why is Melchizedek and king David so special in the sight of God. Consider all those mentioned in the book of Hebrews. They were human just as we are and even though they were not perfect in our understanding it is not mentioned here. God upholds those mentioned in the book of Hebrews as heroes of the gospel. Again, God judges humanity out of His love for Him and through the work of Jesus to purify those who trust in Him. God forgives and forgets. Jesus' shed blood resolves our sins.

Jesus is our way to Salvation and He will redeem His own from the beginning of time until the end of time. The Lord has said He will create a new heart and a right spirit in us. He takes on this responsibility based upon our wiliness to allow Him to do so. I am drawn to point out a quote from the book of Revelation again about the woman named Jezebell. Jesus tells us how He allotted time for her to repent but she refused to do so.

EZEKIEL 11:18-20 KING JAMES VERSION

18 And they shall come thither, and they shall take away all the detestable things thereof and all the abominations thereof from thence.
19 And I will give them one heart, and I will put a new spirit within you; and I will take the stony heart out of their flesh, and will give them an heart of flesh:
20 That they may walk in my statutes, and keep mine ordinances, and do them: and they shall be my people, and I will be their God.

EZEKIEL 36:25-27 KING JAMES VERSION

25 Then will I sprinkle clean water upon you, and ye shall be clean: from all your filthiness, and from all your idols, will I cleanse you.
26 A new heart also will I give you, and a new spirit will I put within you: and I will take away the stony heart out of your flesh, and I will give you an heart of flesh.
27 And I will put my spirit within you, and cause you to walk in my statutes, and ye shall keep my judgments, and do them.

ROMANS 7:5-7 EASY-TO-READ VERSION

5 In the past we were ruled by our sinful selves. The law made us want to do sinful things. And those sinful desires controlled our bodies, so that what we did only brought us spiritual death.
6 In the past the law held us as prisoners, but our old selves died, and we were made free from the law. So now we serve God in a new way, not in the old way, with the written rules. Now we serve God in the new way, with the Spirit.
Our Fight Against Sin

⁷ You might think I am saying that sin and the law are the same. That is not true. But the law was the only way I could learn what sin means. I would never have known it is wrong to want something that is not mine. But the law said, "You must not want what belongs to someone else."[a]
Footnotes
a. Romans 7:7 Quote from Ex. 20:17; Deut. 5:21.

In the same fashion the Lord does the same for all humanity who are willing to repent. It is up to us to accept the work of transformation from a worldly Satan influenced lifestyle (fleshly) to one which is holy and righteous. For those who repent it is granted the privilege to abide with the Lord in heavenly places. For those who refuse they too have a habitation prepared which is loathsome and full of pain and misery.

JOHN 5:28-30 EASY-TO-READ VERSION

²⁸ "Don't be surprised at this. A time is coming when all people who are dead and in their graves will hear his voice.
²⁹ Then they will come out of their graves. Those who did good in this life will rise and have eternal life. But those who did evil will rise to be judged guilty.

³⁰ "I can do nothing alone. I judge only the way I am told. And my judgment is right, because I am not trying to please myself. I want only to please the one who sent me.

PROVERBS 12:1-3 EASY-TO-READ VERSION

¹² Whoever loves discipline loves to learn; whoever hates to be corrected is stupid.
² It is good to learn what pleases the Lord, because he condemns those who plan to do wrong.
³ Evil people are never safe, but good people remain safe and secure.

JUDE 1-10 EASY-TO-READ VERSION

¹ Greetings from Jude, a servant of Jesus Christ and a brother of James.
To those who have been chosen and are loved by God the Father and have been kept safe in Jesus Christ.
² Mercy, peace, and love be yours more and more.
God Will Punish Those Who Do Wrong

³ *Dear friends, I wanted very much to write to you about the salvation we all share together. But I felt the need to write to you about something else: I want to encourage you to fight hard for the faith that God gave his holy people. God gave this faith once, and it is good for all time.*

⁴ *Some people have secretly entered your group. These people have already been judged guilty for what they are doing. Long ago the prophets wrote about them. They are against God. They have used the grace of our God in the wrong way—to do sinful things. They refuse to follow Jesus Christ, our only Master and Lord.*

⁵ *I want to help you remember some things you already know: Remember that the Lord[a] saved his people by bringing them out of the land of Egypt. But later he destroyed all those who did not believe.*

⁶ *And remember the angels who lost their authority to rule. They left their proper home. So the Lord has kept them in darkness, bound with everlasting chains, to be judged on the great day.*

⁷ *Also, remember the cities of Sodom and Gomorrah and the other towns around them. Like those angels they were full of sexual sin and involved themselves in sexual relations that are wrong. And they suffer the punishment of eternal fire, an example for us to see.*

⁸ *It is the same way with these people who have entered your group. They are guided by dreams. They make themselves dirty with sin. They reject God's authority and say bad things against the glorious ones.[b]*

⁹ *Not even the archangel Michael did this. Michael argued with the devil about who would have the body of Moses. But Michael did not dare to condemn even the devil for his false accusations. Instead, Michael said, "The Lord punish you!"*

¹⁰ *But these people criticize things they don't understand. They do understand some things. But they understand these things not by thinking, but by feeling, the way dumb animals understand things. And these are the things that destroy them.*

    Footnotes

        a. Jude 1:5 the Lord Some of the oldest and best Greek manuscripts of Jude have "Jesus" here. If "Jesus" is accepted as the original reading, it should replace "the Lord" in verse 6 as well.

> **b. Jude 1:8 the glorious ones** Literally, *"the glories."*
> *These seem to be some kind of angelic beings.*

Each of us has been given tools to be in this world and not of it. Please put them to use so God can guide us in our life journey. So, live your life to reflect on His work in you and never forget the reason we can do so. It is not by our might nor not by our power but by My Spirit says the Lord. We each are on probation here until the final judgement is pronounced. That is why we are told to live out our lives in fear (respect for Him and trembling) that we do not stumble and by His might and power we will make it. My help comes from the Lord, maker of heaven and earth.

MICAH 7:1-3 EASY-TO-READ VERSION

Micah Is Upset at the Evil People Do
⁷ I am upset because I am like fruit that has been gathered,
  like grapes that have already been picked.
There are no grapes left to eat.
  There are none of the early figs that I love.
² By this I mean that all the faithful people are gone.
  There are no good people left.
Everyone is planning to kill someone.
  Everyone is trying to trap their brother.
³ People are good at doing bad things with both hands.
  Officials ask for bribes.
Judges take money to change their decisions in court.
  "Important leaders" do whatever they want to do.

COLOSSIANS 3 INSPIRED VERSION

Keep Focusing on Christ
¹ If ye then be risen with Christ, seek those things which are above, where Christ sitteth on the right
hand of God.
² Set your affection on things above, not on things on the earth.
3 For ye are dead, and your life is hid with Christ in God.
⁴ When Christ, who is our life, shall appear, then shall ye also appear with him in glory.
Living the New Life
⁵ Mortify therefore your members which are upon the earth; fornication, uncleanness, inordinate
affection, evil concupiscence, and covetousness, which is idolatry;

⁶ *For which things' sake the wrath of God cometh on the children of disobedience;*
⁷ *In the which ye also walked sometime, when ye lived in them.*
⁸ *But now ye also put off all these; anger, wrath, malice, blasphemy, filthy communication out of your mouth.*
⁹ *Lie not one to another, seeing that ye have put off the old man with his deeds;*
¹⁰ *And have put on the new man, which is renewed in knowledge after the image of him that created him;*
¹¹ *Where there is neither Greek nor Jew, circumcision nor uncircumcision, Barbarian, Scythian, bond nor free; but Christ is all, and in all.*
¹² *Put on therefore, as the elect of God, holy and beloved, bowels of mercies, kindness, humbleness of mind, meekness, long-suffering;*
¹³ *Forbearing one another, and forgiving one another, if any man have a quarrel against any; even as Christ forgave you, so also do ye.*
¹⁴ *And above all these things put on charity, which is the bond of perfectness.*
¹⁵ *And let the peace of God rule in your hearts, to the which also ye are called in one body; and be ye thankful.*
¹⁶ *Let the word of Christ dwell in you richly in all wisdom; teaching and admonishing one another in psalms and hymns and spiritual songs, singing with grace in your hearts to the Lord.*
¹⁷ *And whatsoever ye do in word or deed, do all in the name of the Lord Jesus, giving thanks to God and the Father by him.*

Family Duties

¹⁸ *Wives, submit yourselves unto your own husbands, as it is fit in the Lord.*
¹⁹ *Husbands, love your wives, and be not bitter against them.*
²⁰ *Children, obey your parents in all things; for this is well pleasing unto the Lord.*
²¹ *Fathers, provoke not your children to anger, lest they be discouraged.*
²² *Servants, obey in all things your masters according to the flesh; not with eye-service, as menpleasers;*

but in singleness of heart, fearing God;
²³ And whatsoever ye do, do it heartily, as to the Lord, and not unto men;
²⁴ Knowing that of the Lord ye shall receive the reward of the inheritance; for ye serve the Lord Christ.
²⁵ But he that doeth wrong shall receive for the wrong which he hath done; and there is no respect of persons.

COLOSSIANS 4 INSPIRED VERSION

Closing Exhortations
¹ Masters, give unto your servants that which is just and equal; knowing that ye also have a Master in heaven.
² Continue in prayer, and watch in the same with thanksgiving;

REVELATION 3:7-13 KING JAMES VERSION (KJV)

⁷ And to the angel of the Church in Philadelphia write; These things saith he that is holy, he that is true, he that hath the key of David, he that openeth, and no man shutteth; and shutteth, and no man openeth;
⁸ I know thy works: behold, I have set before thee an open door, and no man can shut it: for thou hast a little strength, and hast kept my word, and hast not denied my name.
⁹ Behold, I will make them of the synagogue of Satan, which say they are Jews, and are not, but do lie; behold, I will make them to come and worship before thy feet, and to know that I have loved thee.
¹⁰ Because thou hast kept the word of my patience, I also will keep thee from the hour of temptation, which shall come upon all the world, to try them that dwell upon the earth.
¹¹ Behold, I come quickly: hold that fast which thou hast, that no man take thy crown.
¹² Him that overcometh will I make a pillar in the temple of my God, and he shall go no more out: and I will write upon him the name of my God, and the name of the city of my God, which is new Jerusalem, which cometh down out of heaven from my God: and I will write upon him my new name.
¹³ He that hath an ear, let him hear what the Spirit saith unto the Churches.

ISAIAH 61:10 KING JAMES VERSION

10 I will greatly rejoice in the Lord, my soul shall be joyful in my God; for he hath clothed me with the garments of salvation, he hath covered me with the robe of righteousness, as a bridegroom decketh himself with ornaments, and as a bride adorneth herself with her jewels.

EPHESIANS 6:10-18 KING JAMES VERSION

10 Finally, my brethren, be strong in the Lord, and in the power of his might.
11 Put on the whole armour of God, that ye may be able to stand against the wiles of the devil.
12 For we wrestle not against flesh and blood, but against principalities, against powers, against the rulers of the darkness of this world, against spiritual wickedness in high places.
13 Wherefore take unto you the whole armour of God, that ye may be able to withstand in the evil day, and having done all, to stand.
14 Stand therefore, having your loins girt about with truth, and having on the breastplate of righteousness;
15 And your feet shod with the preparation of the gospel of peace;
16 Above all, taking the shield of faith, wherewith ye shall be able to quench all the fiery darts of the wicked.
17 And take the helmet of salvation, and the sword of the Spirit, which is the word of God:
18 Praying always with all prayer and supplication in the Spirit, and watching thereunto with all perseverance and supplication for all saints;

Does this same decree also apply to us in this day and time to us who follow Him? The greatest witness we can provide is living by kingdom principles.

CHAPTER 8

God Has to Have a Holy and Righteous People to Dwell with Him

PSALM 51:6-12 AMPLIFIED BIBLE

6 Behold, You desire truth in the innermost being,
And in the hidden part [of my heart] You will make me know wisdom.
7 Purify me with [a]hyssop, and I will be clean;
Wash me, and I will be whiter than snow.
8 Make me hear joy and gladness and be satisfied;
Let the bones which You have broken rejoice.
9 Hide Your face from my sins
And blot out all my iniquities.
10 Create in me a clean heart, O God,
And renew a right and steadfast spirit within me.
11 Do not cast me away from Your presence
And do not take Your Holy Spirit from me.
12 Restore to me the joy of Your salvation
And sustain me with a willing spirit.

1 TIMOTHY 1:4-6 KING JAMES VERSION

4 Neither give heed to fables and endless genealogies, which minister questions, rather than godly edifying which is in faith: so do.
5 Now the end of the commandment is charity out of a pure heart, and of a good conscience, and of faith unfeigned:

⁶ From which some having swerved have turned aside unto vain jangling;

1 TIMOTHY 1:4-6 AMPLIFIED BIBLE

⁴ nor to pay attention to legends (fables, myths) and endless genealogies, which give rise to useless speculation and meaningless arguments rather than advancing God's program of instruction which is grounded in faith [and requires surrendering the entire self to God in absolute trust and confidence].
⁵ But the goal of our instruction is love [which springs] from a pure heart and a good conscience and a sincere faith.
⁶ Some individuals have wandered away from these things into empty arguments and useless discussions,

1 PETER 1:21-23 KING JAMES VERSION

²¹ Who by him do believe in God, that raised him up from the dead, and gave him glory; that your faith and hope might be in God.
²² Seeing ye have purified your souls in obeying the truth through the Spirit unto unfeigned love of the brethren, see that ye love one another with a pure heart fervently:
²³ Being born again, not of corruptible seed, but of incorruptible, by the word of God, which liveth and abideth for ever.

COLOSSIANS 3 INSPIRED VERSION

Keep Focusing on Christ
¹ If ye then be risen with Christ, seek those things which are above, where Christ sitteth on the right
hand of God.
² Set your affection on things above, not on things on the earth.
3 For ye are dead, and your life is hid with Christ in God.
⁴ When Christ, who is our life, shall appear, then shall ye also appear with him in glory.
Living the New Life
⁵ Mortify therefore your members which are upon the earth; fornication, uncleanness, inordinate
affection, evil concupiscence, and covetousness, which is idolatry;
⁶ For which things' sake the wrath of God cometh on the children of disobedience;
⁷ In the which ye also walked sometime, when ye lived in them.
⁸ But now ye also put off all these; anger, wrath, malice, blasphemy, filthy communication out of your

mouth.
⁹ Lie not one to another, seeing that ye have put off the old man with his deeds;
¹⁰ And have put on the new man, which is renewed in knowledge after the image of him that created
him;
¹¹ Where there is neither Greek nor Jew, circumcision nor uncircumcision, Barbarian, Scythian, bond
nor free; but Christ is all, and in all.
¹² Put on therefore, as the elect of God, holy and beloved, bowels of mercies, kindness, humbleness of
mind, meekness, long-suffering;
¹³ Forbearing one another, and forgiving one another, if any man have a quarrel against any; even as
Christ forgave you, so also do ye.
¹⁴ And above all these things put on charity, which is the bond of perfectness.
¹⁵ And let the peace of God rule in your hearts, to the which also ye are called in one body; and be ye
thankful.
¹⁶ Let the word of Christ dwell in you richly in all wisdom; teaching and admonishing one another in
psalms and hymns and spiritual songs, singing with grace in your hearts to the Lord.
¹⁷ And whatsoever ye do in word or deed, do all in the name of the Lord Jesus, giving thanks to God
and the Father by him.

Family Duties

¹⁸ Wives, submit yourselves unto your own husbands, as it is fit in the Lord.
¹⁹ Husbands, love your wives, and be not bitter against them.
²⁰ Children, obey your parents in all things; for this is well pleasing unto the Lord.
²¹ Fathers, provoke not your children to anger, lest they be discouraged.
²² Servants, obey in all things your masters according to the flesh; not with eye-service, as menpleasers;
but in singleness of heart, fearing God;
²³ And whatsoever ye do, do it heartily, as to the Lord, and not unto men;
²⁴ Knowing that of the Lord ye shall receive the reward of the inheritance; for ye serve the Lord Christ.

²⁵ But he that doeth wrong shall receive for the wrong which he hath done; and there is no respect of persons.

COLOSSIANS 4:1-2 INSPIRED VERSION

Closing Exhortations
¹ Masters, give unto your servants that which is just and equal; knowing that ye also have a Master in heaven.
² Continue in prayer, and watch in the same with thanksgiving;

EPHESIANS 1:3-11 KING JAMES VERSION

³ Blessed be the God and Father of our Lord Jesus Christ, who hath blessed us with all spiritual blessings in heavenly places in Christ:
⁴ According as he hath chosen us in him before the foundation of the world, that we should be holy and without blame before him in love:
⁵ Having predestinated us unto the adoption of children by Jesus Christ to himself, according to the good pleasure of his will,
⁶ To the praise of the glory of his grace, wherein he hath made us accepted in the beloved.
⁷ In whom we have redemption through his blood, the forgiveness of sins, according to the riches of his grace;
⁸ Wherein he hath abounded toward us in all wisdom and prudence;
⁹ Having made known unto us the mystery of his will, according to his good pleasure which he hath purposed in himself:
¹⁰ That in the dispensation of the fulness of times he might gather together in one all things in Christ, both which are in heaven, and which are on earth; even in him:
¹¹ In whom also we have obtained an inheritance, being predestinated according to the purpose of him who worketh all things after the counsel of his own will:

EPHESIANS 4:11-32 KING JAMES VERSION

¹¹ And he gave some, apostles; and some, prophets; and some, evangelists; and some, pastors and teachers;
¹² For the perfecting of the saints, for the work of the ministry, for the edifying of the body of Christ:
¹³ Till we all come in the unity of the faith, and of the knowledge of the Son of God, unto a perfect man, unto the measure of the stature of the fulness of Christ:

14 That we henceforth be no more children, tossed to and fro, and carried about with every wind of doctrine, by the sleight of men, and cunning craftiness, whereby they lie in wait to deceive;
15 But speaking the truth in love, may grow up into him in all things, which is the head, even Christ:
16 From whom the whole body fitly joined together and compacted by that which every joint supplieth, according to the effectual working in the measure of every part, maketh increase of the body unto the edifying of itself in love.
17 This I say therefore, and testify in the Lord, that ye henceforth walk not as other Gentiles walk, in the vanity of their mind,
18 Having the understanding darkened, being alienated from the life of God through the ignorance that is in them, because of the blindness of their heart:
19 Who being past feeling have given themselves over unto lasciviousness, to work all uncleanness with greediness.
20 But ye have not so learned Christ;
21 If so be that ye have heard him, and have been taught by him, as the truth is in Jesus:
22 That ye put off concerning the former conversation the old man, which is corrupt according to the deceitful lusts;
23 And be renewed in the spirit of your mind;
24 And that ye put on the new man, which after God is created in righteousness and true holiness.
25 Wherefore putting away lying, speak every man truth with his neighbour: for we are members one of another.
26 Be ye angry, and sin not: let not the sun go down upon your wrath:
27 Neither give place to the devil.
28 Let him that stole steal no more: but rather let him labour, working with his hands the thing which is good, that he may have to give to him that needeth.
29 Let no corrupt communication proceed out of your mouth, but that which is good to the use of edifying, that it may minister grace unto the hearers.
30 And grieve not the holy Spirit of God, whereby ye are sealed unto the day of redemption.
31 Let all bitterness, and wrath, and anger, and clamour, and evil speaking, be put away from you, with all malice:
32 And be ye kind one to another, tenderhearted, forgiving one another, even as God for Christ's sake hath forgiven you.

We are told time and time again that God wants us to be pure in heart and spirit not only in the world to come but also on this earth. Yes, the Lord wants us to do all things with love such as His and trust Him for the rest. We are told how the Lord examines the heart of man to determine the reasons behind the choices we have made in this life. All this is based on our acceptance of the work of Jesus and being obedient to the work of the Holy Spirit. We are told that God cannot tolerate sin at all but through the work of Jesus we find forgiveness of sin and a work within us to transform us from the control of the works of darkness to those ordained of God. We are told it is out the heart and conscience of man God sees who we are and what determines our choices. There resides within us a mechanism which stores all that we have done and the reasons behind these. Jesus heals these through forgiveness of sin and instilling within us the liberating gospel of God's pure love. When our reason for performing good works and living a life which glorifies God is motivated by His pure love implanted in our heart then, we are purified and can be allowed to stay in His presence for all eternity. Our performance after we have received the forgiveness of sin dictates how close we can be allowed to be in the presence of the almighty.

JOB 34:11 EASY-TO-READ VERSION

[11] He pays us back for what we have done.
He gives us what we deserve.

ROMANS 2:1-6 EASY-TO-READ VERSION

Let God Be the Judge
[1] So do you think that you can judge those other people? You are wrong. You too are guilty of sin. You judge them, but you do the same things they do. So when you judge them, you are really condemning yourself.
[2] God judges all who do such things, and we know his judgment is right.
[3] And since you do the same things as those people you judge, surely you understand that God will punish you too. How could you think you would be able to escape his judgment?
[4] God has been kind to you. He has been very patient, waiting for you to change. But you think nothing of his kindness. Maybe you

don't understand that God is kind to you so that you will decide to change your lives.

⁵ But you are so stubborn! You refuse to change. So you are making your own punishment greater and greater. You will be punished on the day when God will show his anger. On that day everyone will see how right God is to judge people.

⁶ He will reward or punish everyone for what they have done.

2 Corinthians 3:17-18 King James Version

¹⁷ Now the Lord is that Spirit: and where the Spirit of the Lord is, there is liberty.

¹⁸ But we all, with open face beholding as in a glass the glory of the Lord, are changed into the same image from glory to glory, even as by the Spirit of the Lord.

1 CORINTHIANS 15:35-42 KING JAMES VERSION

³⁵ But some man will say, How are the dead raised up? and with what body do they come?

³⁶ Thou fool, that which thou sowest is not quickened, except it die:

³⁷ And that which thou sowest, thou sowest not that body that shall be, but bare grain, it may chance of wheat, or of some other grain:

³⁸ But God giveth it a body as it hath pleased him, and to every seed his own body.

³⁹ All flesh is not the same flesh: but there is one kind of flesh of men, another flesh of beasts, another of fishes, and another of birds.

⁴⁰ There are also celestial bodies, and bodies terrestrial: but the glory of the celestial is one, and the glory of the terrestrial is another.

⁴¹ There is one glory of the sun, and another glory of the moon, and another glory of the stars: for one star differeth from another star in glory.

⁴² So also is the resurrection of the dead. It is sown in corruption; it is raised in incorruption:

REVELATION 2:19-21 EASY-TO-READ VERSION

¹⁹ "I know what you do. I know about your love, your faith, your service, and your patience. I know that you are doing more now than you did at first.

²⁰ But I have this against you: You let that woman Jezebel do what she wants. She says that she is a prophet,[a] but she is leading my

people away with her teaching. Jezebel leads my people to commit sexual sins and to eat food that is offered to idols.
[21] I have given her time to change her heart and turn away from her sin, but she does not want to change.
Footnotes
    a. *Revelation 2:20 prophet Jezebel was a false prophet. She claimed to speak for God, but she didn't really speak God's truth.*

The blood of the lamb covers our sin which we repent from but if we want to continue in this filth the Lord allows us to be true to our choice just as Jezebel which was recorded in the book of Revelation.

We see in the book of Revelation the strange creatures which circle the throne of God in the scripture whose faces show that all His creation man and beast were made to shout glory to the highest. Even in our fallen state God still loves us enough to prepare a way for us to avoid that dreaded eternal death. So, He has established a way for us to avoid this if we so choose. Man, it is the Lord's pure love which allows us to repent and choose to denounce Satan's lifestyle and choose righteousness. We are not forced into it or cloned into being like the Lord. He has the power to do this. The Lord loves us enough to grant us the right to accept or reject the offer of release from all or part of the bondage of sin so that we can live a life of true love and holiness.

EXODUS 19:5-7 AMPLIFIED BIBLE

[5] Now therefore, if you will in fact obey My voice and keep My covenant (agreement), then you shall be My own special possession and treasure from among all peoples [of the world], for all the earth is Mine;
[6] and you shall be to Me a kingdom of priests and a holy nation [set apart for My purpose].' These are the words that you shall speak to the Israelites."
[7] So Moses called for the elders of the people, and told them all these words which the Lord commanded him.

EPHESIANS 1:3-5 KING JAMES VERSION

[3] Blessed be the God and Father of our Lord Jesus Christ, who hath blessed us with all spiritual blessings in heavenly places in Christ:

4 *According as he hath chosen us in him before the foundation of the world, that we should be holy and without blame before him in love:*
5 *Having predestinated us unto the adoption of children by Jesus Christ to himself, according to the good pleasure of his will,*

EPHESIANS 2:20-22 AMPLIFIED BIBLE

20 *having been built on the foundation of the apostles and prophets, with Christ Jesus Himself as the [chief] Cornerstone,*
21 *in whom the whole structure is joined together, and it continues [to increase] growing into a holy temple in the Lord [a sanctuary dedicated, set apart, and sacred to the presence of the Lord].*
22 *In Him [and in fellowship with one another] you also are being built together into a dwelling place of God in the Spirit.*

EPHESIANS 5:26-27 KING JAMES VERSION

26 *That he might sanctify and cleanse it with the washing of water by the word,*
27 *That he might present it to himself a glorious church, not having spot, or wrinkle, or any such thing; but that it should be holy and without blemish.*

So many do not understand the gravity of the choice they make to live a worldly life ruled by our selfish desires which have been influenced by Satan. We are blind to the fact that by continuing to follow the same old patterns acquired in this life we are being led to the pit of hell. Yes, the old saying holds true. "If you keep doing the same things you will get the same result." So, the good news of the gospel is that He loves us enough to forgive the sins of the past and has made a way for us to escape the punishment which is dictated by the breaking the law of loving God and our neighbor in the same way He loves us.

In scripture and everyday life, The Lord has provided instructions from Him so that we can choose life and not punishment for our sinful lifestyle. So many have been led to believe the lies which are part of our everyday life as good for us. Take for instance the fact that we are told we deserve to be pampered in this life by gathering as much as we can for ourselves. We seek Self-gratification as our goal, and we believe that we deserve to have it. Repeatedly we are told how greed is sinful in scripture. Yet we yield to the premise to experience or get what we can now or we will never have another chance to experience it again.

Summary

Even though the prophecy titled Ephesians is not exceptionally long, it carries such power. In this I find the answer to something which I have struggled with all my Christian life which is, why bad things happen to good people? I now have an answer to this question. Satan's goal is to kill steal and destroy all goodness and our ability to receive the love of the Lord.

I am led to point to the church at Smyrna. This was a group of mature Christians. They had been introduced to the Lord, just as the Pentecost Saints, with the spirit of Jesus. He was able to tell them things that baby Christians could not understand. They had received the strength only Godly love can provide. The words, Jesus spoke to them in the book of Revelations glorify and honor God. Those who composed the church at Smyrna knew, without a doubt, that they had all the power of the Godhead in them, and they knew even death could not defeat the ultimate purpose of Jesus. Accepting Jesus as our savior and truly repenting provides us eternal life and allows His plan to be fulfilled in us. We, just as the church at Smyrna, knew that our sins is washed by the blood of the Lamb when we truly repent and we can stand before God in confidence knowing we will hear the words "well done my good and faithful servants". Don't we all desire to have confidence that we will hear these words when we stand before God for final judgement?

REVELATION 2:8-11 AMPLIFIED BIBLE

Message to Smyrna
8 *"And to the angel (divine messenger) of the church in [a]Smyrna write:*
"These are the words of the First and the Last [absolute Deity, the Son of God] who died and came to life [again]:
9 *'I know your suffering and your poverty (but you are rich), and how you are blasphemed and slandered by those who say they*

are Jews and are not, but are a synagogue of Satan [they are Jews only by blood, and do not believe and truly honor the God whom they claim to worship].

[10] Fear nothing that you are about to suffer. Be aware that the devil is about to throw some of you into prison, that you may be tested [in your faith], and for ten days you will have tribulation. Be faithful to the point of death [if you must die for your faith], and I will give you the crown [consisting] of life.

[11] He who has an ear, let him hear and heed what the Spirit says to the churches. He who overcomes [the world through believing that Jesus is the Son of God] will not be hurt by the second death ([b]the lake of fire).'

Footnotes

a. Revelation 2:8 In ancient times Smyrna (modern Izmir, Turkey) was a beautiful, cosmopolitan city. Located on the Aegean coast, it vied with Ephesus and Pergamum in importance in Asia Minor. It was closely identified with Rome and the cult of emperor worship. Smyrna was later the home of Polycarp, the great Christian church leader who, at the age of eighty-six, was burned at the stake for his refusal to worship the Roman emperor.

b. Revelation 2:11 The Valley of Hinnom located south of Jerusalem was the place where garbage burned continuously. Often regarded in ancient times as symbolic of hell (the lake of fire), reserved for the wicked. Paradise or Abraham's bosom (cf Luke 16:22) was the place reserved for the good in anticipation of heaven. Mentioned in Matt 5:22, 29, 30; 10:28; 18:9; 23:15, 33; Mark 9:43, 45, 47; Luke 12:5; James 3:6.

MATTHEW 25:20-22 KING JAMES VERSION (KJV)

[20] And so he that had received five talents came and brought other five talents, saying, Lord, thou deliveredst unto me five talents: behold, I have gained beside them five talents more.

[21] His lord said unto him, Well done, thou good and faithful servant: thou hast been faithful over a few things, I will make thee ruler over many things: enter thou into the joy of thy lord.

[22] He also that had received two talents came and said, Lord, thou deliveredst unto me two talents: behold, I have gained two other talents beside them.

JOHN 14:21 EASY-TO-READ VERSION

²¹ Those who really love me are the ones who not only know my commands but also obey them. My Father will love such people, and I will love them. I will make myself known to them."

What are we to gain from this portion of this prophecy?
1. Here we see that God is demonstrating through our faithfulness that His wisdom is above that of His greatest adversary, the devil and that of man.
2. The trials we face are presented to all. Yet they are more than a thorn in our side. They are for the glory of God.
3. Each successful overcoming of a trial is a representation to the devil and all opposition to God that the wisdom of God is supreme and cannot be frustrated.
4. All Christians will have to face temptations but we have an audience with God who provides a way around these.
5. As stated before, He stands with us in all trials.
6. Trials are proof that God is right. He will provide the strength we need to overcome them. Trials will come in many forms, so we need to be equipped to handle them.
7. When we become mature Christians Jesus can talk to us as adults not as babes constantly having to repent.
8. Jesus is in control. It is Jesus and only Jesus who has control over salvation and entry into eternal life. Only Jesus can prevent this. It is He who judges when and how the way is opened or closed. He sets the conditions, no one else.

Ephesians 4:23-25 Amplified Bible

²³ and be continually renewed in the spirit of your mind [having a fresh, untarnished mental and spiritual attitude],
²⁴ and put on the new self [the regenerated and renewed nature], created in God's image, [godlike] in the righteousness and holiness of the truth [living in a way that expresses to God your gratitude for your salvation].
²⁵ Therefore, rejecting all falsehood [whether lying, defrauding, telling half-truths, spreading rumors, any such as these], speak truth each one with his neighbor, for we are all parts of one another [and we are all parts of the body of Christ].

John 14:5-7 Amplified Bible

> [5] *Thomas said to Him, "Lord, we do not know where You are going; so how can we know the way?"*
> [6] *Jesus said to him, "[a]I am the [only] Way [to God] and the [real] Truth and the [real] Life; no one comes to the Father but through Me.*
> **Jesus' Oneness with the Father**
> [7] *If you had [really] known Me, you would also have known My Father. From now on you know Him, and have seen Him."*
> **Footnotes**
> > a. John 14:6 The sixth of the memorable "I am" statements. See note 6:35.

9. All have this open opportunity. It up to us to accept the offer or not.
10. When we are truly converted and accepted and have been transformed into duplicating the Love of God, we will have the courage needed to face anything. As mature Christians we will not fear any circumstance which stands before us.
11. Understand that perfect love within us from the Godhead is our shield against all situations which the devil can toss at us.
12. The offer of salvation carries conditions which we are to adhere to. These are.
    a. Admit our sins and confess them.
    b. We need to be willing to accept the way of life we have now is not acceptable and is guided by the world views under the influence of Satan; with Christ this can be changed. Jesus will help us by freeing us from the sinful life we now live to adopt one of righteousness.
    c. Admit that Jesus loves me enough to accept me as I am and makes the pact that He will take on the task of creating a new Heart and renewed spirit in us.

> **Psalm 51:9-11 Amplified Bible**
> [9] *Hide Your face from my sins*
> *And blot out all my iniquities.*
> [10] *Create in me a clean heart, O God,*
> *And renew a right and steadfast spirit within me.*
> [11] *Do not cast me away from Your presence*
> *And do not take Your Holy Spirit from me.*

d. We need to accept that Jesus provides the Holy Spirit to guide and teach us how to be set free from the sinful self which we once followed.

> **Acts 15:8-10 Easy-to-Read Version**
> **8** God knows everyone, even their thoughts, and he accepted these non-Jewish people. He showed this to us by giving them the Holy Spirit the same as he did to us.
> **9** To God, those people are not different from us. When they believed, God made their hearts pure.
> **10** So now, why are you putting a heavy burden[a] around the necks of the non-Jewish followers of Jesus? Are you trying to make God angry? We and our fathers were not able to carry that burden.
> Footnotes
> a. Acts 15:10 burden The Jewish law. Some of the Jews tried to make the non-Jewish believers follow this law.

e. Jesus states we must agree to follow His commandments which are all included in what He identifies as two: Love God and Love our neighbor as ourselves.

> **John 14:14-16 Easy-to-Read Version**
> **14** If you ask me for anything in my name, I will do it.
> The Promise of the Holy Spirit
> **15** "If you love me, you will do what I command.
> **16** I will ask the Father, and he will give you another Helper[a] to be with you forever.
> Footnotes
> a. John 14:16 Helper Or "Comforter," the Holy Spirit (see "Holy Spirit" in the Word List). Also in verse 26.

f. Accept that Jesus provides spiritual forgiveness of all sin. We are to accept that we must endure the consequences of our earthly sins.

g. Accept that Jesus wants us to exhibit a reformed lifestyle. One that shows as much as possible we are doing the righteous works for which we are created.

Utmost in this is how we are called to accept and treat each other and come to agreement on Him and His teachings for we are one in Him and each with one faith one gospel one hope and one salvation.

Ephesians 4:31-32 Easy-to-Read Version
³¹ Never be bitter, angry, or mad. Never shout angrily or say things to hurt others. Never do anything evil.
³² Be kind and loving to each other. Forgive each other the same as God forgave you through Christ.

h. He states this is how you will know my disciples is that they have love for one another.

John 13:34-36 King James Version
³⁴ A new commandment I give unto you, That ye love one another; as I have loved you, that ye also love one another.
³⁵ By this shall all men know that ye are my disciples, if ye have love one to another.
³⁶ Simon Peter said unto him, Lord, whither goest thou? Jesus answered him, Whither I go, thou canst not follow me now; but thou shalt follow me afterwards.

John 15:10-18 Easy-to-Read Version
¹⁰ I have obeyed my Father's commands, and he continues to love me. In the same way, if you obey my commands, I will continue to love you.
¹¹ I have told you these things so that you can have the true happiness that I have. I want you to be completely happy.
¹² This is what I command you: Love each other as I have loved you.
¹³ The greatest love people can show is to die for their friends.
¹⁴ You are my friends if you do what I tell you to do.
¹⁵ I no longer call you servants, because servants don't know what their master is doing. But now I call you friends, because I have told you everything that my Father told me.
¹⁶ "You did not choose me. I chose you. And I gave you this work: to go and produce fruit—fruit that will last.

Then the Father will give you anything you ask for in my name.
17 This is my command: Love each other.
Jesus Warns His Followers
18 "If the world hates you, remember that they hated me first.

i. We are to call upon the Holy Spirit to lead us into all truth and transformation from sinful to righteous principles and from fleshly love to God's pure Love.

John 16:12-14 Easy-to-Read Version
12 "I have so much more to tell you, but it is too much for you to accept now.
13 But when the Spirit of truth comes, he will lead you into all truth. He will not speak his own words. He will speak only what he hears and will tell you what will happen in the future.
14 The Spirit of truth will bring glory to me by telling you what he receives from me.

Romans 6:18-23 Easy-to-Read Version
18 You were made free from sin, and now you are slaves to what is right.
19 I use this example from everyday life because you need help in understanding spiritual truths. In the past you offered the parts of your body to be slaves to your immoral and sinful thoughts. The result was that you lived only for sin. In the same way, you must now offer yourselves to be slaves to what is right. Then you will live only for God.
20 In the past you were slaves to sin, and you did not even think about doing right.
21 You did evil things, and now you are ashamed of what you did. Did those things help you? No, they only brought death.
22 But now you are free from sin. You have become slaves of God, and the result is that you live only for God. This will bring you eternal life.
23 When people sin, they earn what sin pays—death. But God gives his people a free gift—eternal life in Christ Jesus our Lord.

Romans 6:15-23 Easy-to-Read Version
Slaves of Goodness

WHAT GOD IS SAYING IN THE BOOK OF EPHESIANS • 141

¹⁵ *So what should we do? Should we sin because we are under grace and not under law? Certainly not!*
¹⁶ *Surely you know that you become the slaves of whatever you give yourselves to. Anything or anyone you follow will be your master. You can follow sin, or you can obey God. Following sin brings spiritual death, but obeying God makes you right with him.*
¹⁷ *In the past you were slaves to sin—sin controlled you. But thank God, you fully obeyed what you were taught.*
¹⁸ *You were made free from sin, and now you are slaves to what is right.*
¹⁹ *I use this example from everyday life because you need help in understanding spiritual truths. In the past you offered the parts of your body to be slaves to your immoral and sinful thoughts. The result was that you lived only for sin. In the same way, you must now offer yourselves to be slaves to what is right. Then you will live only for God.*
²⁰ *In the past you were slaves to sin, and you did not even think about doing right.*
²¹ *You did evil things, and now you are ashamed of what you did. Did those things help you? No, they only brought death.*
²² *But now you are free from sin. You have become slaves of God, and the result is that you live only for God. This will bring you eternal life.*
²³ *When people sin, they earn what sin pays—death. But God gives his people a free gift—eternal life in Christ Jesus our Lord.*

j. We are to call upon the Holy Spirit to help us understand scripture and to be able to use it in our walk with Jesus and with each other. He will teach us how sinful behavior leads to death and how God is and will and has been performing the work to call us to reject sin and accept righteousness.

Ephesians 3:4-6 Easy-to-Read Version
⁴ *And if you read what I wrote, you can see that I understand the secret truth about Christ.*

⁵ People who lived in other times were not told that secret truth. But now, through the Spirit, God has made it known to his holy apostles and prophets.
⁶ And this is the secret truth: that by hearing the Good News, those who are not Jews will share with the Jews in the blessings God has for his people. They are part of the same body, and they share in the promise God made through Christ Jesus.

Ephesians 5:8-10 King James Version
⁸ For ye were sometimes darkness, but now are ye light in the Lord: walk as children of light:
⁹ (For the fruit of the Spirit is in all goodness and righteousness and truth;)
¹⁰ Proving what is acceptable unto the Lord.

k. We need to accept that Jesus provides us with the gift of eternal life which saves us from the eternal death which awaits those who do not accept His offer of salvation.

l. We need to accept all our righteousness is provided through Jesus.

Romans 3:21-23 Amplified Bible
Justification by Faith
²¹ But now the righteousness of God has been clearly revealed [independently and completely] apart from the Law, though it is [actually] confirmed by the Law and the [words and writings of the] Prophets.
²² This righteousness of God comes through faith in Jesus Christ for all those [Jew or Gentile] who believe [and trust in Him and acknowledge Him as God's Son]. There is no distinction,
²³ since all have sinned and continually fall short of the glory of God,

m. Jesus will share powers from on High when we can be trusted to use them righteously under the guidance of the Holy Spirit learning the use of these also as shown in scripture.

n. Jesus will heal us physically and spiritually as the Father directs to glorify Them and not our selfish desires.

o. Jesus stands as our representative before God and the entire world and our defense against the devil and His sinful influence.
p. It is through Jesus we are granted fellowship with Father God.
q. Jesus is in control of all spiritual gifts and all angelic ministries.
r. Paul was inspired to provide details as to how we should treat each other, and these are true indicators of those who have genuinely repented.
s. Paul was appointed to teach us how to live a Christ like life which he points out as being kind to one another patient with one another and even goes as far as to define love and its characteristic traits.
t. Jesus uses the apostle John to point out in the book of Revelation what He expects from us as His followers. See the first three chapters written to the seven churches.
u. Yes, Jesus loves us with a love which is unconditional but the aspect of being a His disciples comes with expectations which are how we are called to live in a renewed relationship with Him and each other.

CHAPTER 9

Jesus Who He is and His Love and His Purpose

EPHESIANS 1:1-14 KING JAMES VERSION

¹ Paul, an apostle of Jesus Christ by the will of God, to the saints which are at Ephesus, and to the faithful in Christ Jesus:
² Grace be to you, and peace, from God our Father, and from the Lord Jesus Christ.
³ Blessed be the God and Father of our Lord Jesus Christ, who hath blessed us with all spiritual blessings in heavenly places in Christ:
⁴ According as he hath chosen us in him before the foundation of the world, that we should be holy and without blame before him in love:
⁵ Having predestinated us unto the adoption of children by Jesus Christ to himself, according to the good pleasure of his will,
⁶ To the praise of the glory of his grace, wherein he hath made us accepted in the beloved.
⁷ In whom we have redemption through his blood, the forgiveness of sins, according to the riches of his grace;
⁸ Wherein he hath abounded toward us in all wisdom and prudence;
⁹ Having made known unto us the mystery of his will, according to his good pleasure which he hath purposed in himself:
¹⁰ That in the dispensation of the fulness of times he might gather together in one all things in Christ, both which are in heaven, and which are on earth; even in him:
¹¹ In whom also we have obtained an inheritance, being predestinated according to the purpose of him who worketh all things after the counsel of his own will:

¹² *That we should be to the praise of his glory, who first trusted in Christ.*
¹³ *In whom ye also trusted, after that ye heard the word of truth, the gospel of your salvation: in whom also after that ye believed, ye were sealed with that holy Spirit of promise,*
¹⁴ *Which is the earnest of our inheritance until the redemption of the purchased possession, unto the praise of his glory.*

EPHESIANS 5:1-2 KING JAMES VERSION

¹ *Be ye therefore followers of God, as dear children;*
² *And walk in love, as Christ also hath loved us, and hath given himself for us an offering and a sacrifice to God for a sweetsmelling savour.*

EPHESIANS 6:5-6 KING JAMES VERSION

⁵ *Servants, be obedient to them that are your masters according to the flesh, with fear and trembling, in singleness of your heart, as unto Christ;*
⁶ *Not with eyeservice, as menpleasers; but as the servants of Christ, doing the will of God from the heart;*
⁷ *With good will doing service, as to the Lord, and not to men:*
⁸ *Knowing that whatsoever good thing any man doeth, the same shall he receive of the Lord, whether he be bond or free.*

It is plainly stated here that Jesus is the Son of God. Paul is led to identify several different responsibilities which He has, and He addresses Him as our Lord. We see from this scripture Jesus existed before all things were created. We are told that Christ was chosen before the foundation of the world. So, we can understand that Jesus and His role was established before the world was created. The word foundation is used in the scripture but if we search older scripture, we find that in the creation of the world and humanity there is reference to more than one person taking part in the creation. Refer to Gensis here we find such references.

Genesis 1:1-3 Easy-to-Read Version
The Beginning of the World
¹ *God created the sky and the earth. At first,*
² *the earth was completely empty. There was nothing on the earth. Darkness covered the ocean, and God's Spirit moved over[a] the water.*
The First Day—Light

> ³ Then God said, "Let there be light!" And light began to shine.[b]
> Footnotes
>> a. Genesis 1:2 moved over The Hebrew word means "to fly over" or "to swoop down," like a bird flying over its nest to protect its babies.
>> b. Genesis 1:3 Or "In the beginning, God created the heavens and the earth. While 2 the earth had no special shape, and darkness covered the ocean, and God's Spirit hovered over the water, 3 God said, 'Let there be light,' and there was light." Or "When God began to create the sky and the earth, 2 while the earth was completely empty, and darkness covered the ocean, and a powerful wind blew over the water, 3 God said, 'Let there be light,' and there was light."

I am assured that we will also find such references in the biblical books and works which we do not have at this time.

Jesus is God's choice for all things having to do with the church. It is under His choice to manage and to assure that it meets the intents and purposes which God has established. All this Jesus does in compliance with God's desires.

> **Ephesians 1:2-4 Easy-to-Read Version**
> ² Grace and peace to you from God our Father and the Lord Jesus Christ.
> **Spiritual Blessings in Christ**
> ³ Praise be to the God and Father of our Lord Jesus Christ. In Christ, God has given us every spiritual blessing in heaven.
> ⁴ In Christ, he chose us before the world was made. He chose us in love to be his holy people—people who could stand before him without any fault.
> **Ephesians 1:19-23 Easy-to-Read Version**
> ¹⁹ And you will know that God's power is very great for us who believe. It is the same as the mighty power
> ²⁰ he used to raise Christ from death and put him at his right side in the heavenly places.
> ²¹ He put Christ over all rulers, authorities, powers, and kings. He gave him authority over everything that has power in this world or in the next world.
> ²² God put everything under Christ's power and made him head over everything for the church.

> ²³ The church is Christ's body. It is filled with him. He makes everything complete in every way.
>
> *Ephesians 3:20-21 Easy-to-Read Version*
> ²⁰ With God's power working in us, he can do much, much more than anything we can ask or think of.
> ²¹ To him be glory in the church and in Christ Jesus for all time, forever and ever. Amen.
>
> *Ephesians 5:22-24 Easy-to-Read Version*
> ²² Wives, be willing to serve your husbands the same as the Lord.
> ²³ A husband is the head of his wife, just as Christ is the head of the church. Christ is the Savior of the church, which is his body.
> ²⁴ The church serves under Christ, so it is the same with you wives. You should be willing to serve your husbands in everything.
>
> *Ephesians 5:28-30 Easy-to-Read Version*
> ²⁸ And husbands should love their wives like that. They should love their wives as they love their own bodies. The man who loves his wife loves himself,
> ²⁹ because no one ever hates his own body, but feeds and takes care of it. And that is what Christ does for the church
> ³⁰ because we are parts of his body.

Jesus sets the example of what it means to live a Godly life in an ungodly world. He proved that it is possible to be in this world and not a part of it. We on the other hand must learn that our lives need to be restructured to be the same as Jesus. That is why He made the statement that we must be born again.

> *John 3:6-21 Easy-to-Read Version*
> ⁶ The only life people get from their human parents is physical. But the new life that the Spirit gives a person is spiritual.
> ⁷ Don't be surprised that I told you, 'You must be born again.'
> ⁸ The wind blows wherever it wants to. You hear it, but you don't know where it is coming from or where it is going. It is the same with everyone who is born from the Spirit."
> ⁹ Nicodemus asked, "How is all this possible?"
> ¹⁰ Jesus said, "You are an important teacher of Israel, and you still don't understand these things?
> ¹¹ The truth is, we talk about what we know. We tell about what we have seen. But you people don't accept what we tell you.
> ¹² I have told you about things here on earth, but you do not believe me. So I'm sure you will not believe me if I tell you about heavenly things!

¹³ The only one who has ever gone up to heaven is the one who came down from heaven—the Son of Man.
¹⁴ "Moses lifted up the snake in the desert.[a] It is the same with the Son of Man. He must be lifted up too.
¹⁵ Then everyone who believes in him can have eternal life."[b]
¹⁶ Yes, God loved the world so much that he gave his only Son, so that everyone who believes in him would not be lost but have eternal life.
¹⁷ God sent his Son into the world. He did not send him to judge the world guilty, but to save the world through him.
¹⁸ People who believe in God's Son are not judged guilty. But people who do not believe are already judged, because they have not believed in God's only Son.
¹⁹ They are judged by this fact: The light[c] has come into the world. But they did not want light. They wanted darkness, because they were doing evil things.
²⁰ Everyone who does evil hates the light. They will not come to the light, because the light will show all the bad things they have done. ²¹ But anyone who follows the true way comes to the light. Then the light will show that whatever they have done was done through God.

Footnotes
   a. John 3:14 Moses lifted ... desert When God's people were dying from snake bites, God told Moses to put a brass snake on a pole for them to look at and be healed. See Num. 21:4-9.
   b. John 3:15 Some scholars think that Jesus' words to Nicodemus continue through verse 21.
   c. John 3:19 light This means Christ, the Word, who brought to the world understanding about God.

Everything Paul is led to share about what it takes to live a Christ like life on earth is spelled out in the book of Ephesians. It is the new life in Christ which Jesus has Paul to describe in this work. Here we find that Jesus is the author and finisher of our faith. That is, Jesus is working through the Holy Spirit. Jesus provides us with the knowledge of what He requires and those changes we need to make to be the "right stuff" to live a transformed life on earth. This is so Jesus can make all things one. That is so that Jesus can bring about the same conditions on both heaven and earth. Jesus is the one whom God has ordained for the task of doing the necessary work to change us from being controlled by the evil powers on high (the evil princes of the air). Jesus works to have us shed these influences and be transformed to a new life dedicated to living according to the principles of God. We are to absorb Father God's righteousness which will replace the devilish or evil character which we have absorbed here on earth. The Lord has an awesome task which on the surface may seem impossible but to God all things are possible.

> **Mark 9:20-24 Easy-to-Read Version**
> **20 So the followers brought the boy to Jesus. When the evil spirit saw Jesus, it attacked the boy. The boy fell down and rolled on the ground. He was foaming at the mouth.**
> **21 Jesus asked the boy's father, "How long has this been happening to him?"**
> **The father answered, "Since he was very young.**
> **22 The spirit often throws him into a fire or into water to kill him. If you can do anything, please have pity on us and help us."**
> **23 Jesus said to the father, "Why did you say 'if you can'? All things are possible for the one who believes."**
> **24 Immediately the father shouted, "I do believe. Help me to believe more!"**

This includes changing what we would consider a worthless individual into the person God created us to be. The Lord created us to do good works and match His divine nature. The Lord wants us to have a new Godly lifestyle rather than the devilish nature we have lived in this life.

God says here in the book of Ephesians that it is Jesus whom He has entrusted to perform the task of building His kingdom here on earth just as it is in heaven. It is stated this way in scripture.

> **Matthew 18:18-20 Easy-to-Read Version**
> **18 "I can assure you that when you speak judgment here on earth, it will be God's judgment. And when you promise forgiveness here on earth, it will be God's forgiveness.[a]**
> **19 To say it another way, if two of you on earth agree on anything you pray for, my Father in heaven will do what you ask.**
> **20 Yes, if two or three people are together believing in me, I am there with them."**
> **Footnotes**
> > a. Matthew 18:18 when you speak ... God's forgiveness Literally, "whatever you bind on earth will have been

bound in heaven, and whatever you loose on earth will have been loosed in heaven."

Jesus has been entrusted with handling everything that has to do with structuring and building the church. We are the church not buildings, organizations, or creeds. It is the essence of our spiritual makeup which is the true church and Jesus has been entrusted with this responsibility. It is not something we do on our own, but it is by His transforming efforts working in unity with the Holy Spirit which empowers us to be recreated into what God desires for us to be. This is grace in its true sense. It is Jesus and God working in us to be the unblemished church; those individuals whom are acceptable to abide with God in heaven.

Ephesians 5:20-28 Amplified Bible
[20] always giving thanks to God the Father for all things, in the name of our Lord Jesus Christ; 21 being subject to one another out of reverence for Christ.
Marriage Like Christ and the Church
[22] Wives, be subject [a]to your own husbands, as [a service] to the Lord.
[23] For the husband is head of the wife, as Christ is head of the church, Himself being the Savior of the body.
[24] But as the church is subject to Christ, so also wives should be subject to their husbands in everything [respecting both their position as protector and their responsibility to God as head of the house].
[25] Husbands, love your wives [seek the highest good for her and surround her with a caring, unselfish love], just as Christ also loved the church and gave Himself up for her,
[26] so that He might sanctify the church, having cleansed her by the washing of water with the word [of God],
[27] so that [in turn] He might present the church to Himself in glorious splendor, without spot or wrinkle or any such thing; but that she would be holy [set apart for God] and blameless.
[28] Even so husbands should and are morally obligated to love their own wives as [being in a sense] their own bodies. He who loves his own wife loves himself.
Footnotes
    a. Ephesians 5:22 The wife to her husband, not to men in general; not as inferior to him, nor in violation of her Christian ethics, but honoring her husband as

> protector and head of the home, respecting the responsibility of his position and his accountability to God.
>
> ### Matthew 16:15-19 Easy-to-Read Version
> ¹⁵ Then Jesus said to his followers, "And who do you say I am?"
> ¹⁶ Simon Peter answered, "You are the Messiah, the Son of the living God."
> ¹⁷ Jesus answered, "You are blessed, Simon son of Jonah. No one taught you that. My Father in heaven showed you who I am.
> ¹⁸ So I tell you, you are Peter.[a] And I will build my church on this rock. The power of death[b] will not be able to defeat my church.
> ¹⁹ I will give you the keys to God's kingdom. When you speak judgment here on earth, that judgment will be God's judgment. When you promise forgiveness here on earth, that forgiveness will be God's forgiveness."[c]
>
> Footnotes
> a. Matthew 16:18 Peter The Greek name "Peter," like the Aramaic name "Cephas," means "rock."
> b. Matthew 16:18 power of death Literally, "gates of Hades."
> c. Matthew 16:19 When you speak ... God's forgiveness Literally, "Whatever you bind on earth will have been bound in heaven, and whatever you loose on earth will have been loosed in heaven."

What an awesome responsibility Jesus has accepted. Yet He is more than capable to perform this work. Jesus has outlined the attributes which he wants to have us not only emulate but to become part of who we are.

We are told that Jesus was the one chosen to perform the work of creating all things.

> ### Ephesians 3:8-10 Easy-to-Read Version
> ⁸ I am the least important of all God's people. But he gave me this gift—to tell the non-Jewish people the Good News about the riches Christ has. These riches are too great to understand fully.
> ⁹ And God gave me the work of telling all people about the plan for his secret truth. That secret truth has been hidden in him since the beginning of time. He is the one who created everything.
> ¹⁰ His purpose was that all the rulers and powers in the heavenly places will now know the many different ways he shows his wisdom. They will know this because of the church.

Ephesians 2:8-11 Easy-to-Read Version

⁸ I mean that you have been saved by grace because you believed. You did not save yourselves; it was a gift from God.

⁹ You are not saved by the things you have done, so there is nothing to boast about.

¹⁰ God has made us what we are. In Christ Jesus, God made us new people so that we would spend our lives doing the good things he had already planned for us to do.

One in Christ

¹¹ You were not born as Jews. You are the people the Jews call "uncircumcised.[a]" Those Jews who call you "uncircumcised" call themselves "circumcised." (Their circumcision is only something they themselves do to their bodies.)

Footnotes
  a. Ephesians 2:11 uncircumcised People not having the mark of circumcision like the Jews have.

Hebrews 8:9-11 King James Version

⁹ Not according to the covenant that I made with their fathers in the day when I took them by the hand to lead them out of the land of Egypt; because they continued not in my covenant, and I regarded them not, saith the Lord.

¹⁰ For this is the covenant that I will make with the house of Israel after those days, saith the Lord; I will put my laws into their mind, and write them in their hearts: and I will be to them a God, and they shall be to me a people:

¹¹ And they shall not teach every man his neighbour, and every man his brother, saying, Know the Lord: for all shall know me, from the least to the greatest.

Hebrews 8:9-11 Easy-to-Read Version

⁹ It will not be like the agreement
  that I gave to their fathers.
That is the agreement I gave when I took them by the hand
  and led them out of Egypt.
They did not continue following the agreement I gave them,
  and I turned away from them, says the Lord.

¹⁰ This is the new agreement I will give the people of Israel.
  I will give this agreement in the future, says the Lord:
I will put my laws in their minds,
  and I will write my laws on their hearts.
I will be their God,
  and they will be my people.

¹¹ Never again will anyone have to teach their neighbors

> or their family to know the Lord.
> All people—the greatest and the least important—will know me.

He is the one who established the laws or parameters by which all things function. He set in motion the solar system. He established how the moon's gravity pull impacts ocean currents. He set up the water cycle. He put in motion the planets and the life cycle of the suns in the different solar systems. He set up the laws by which atoms and their components interact. He established the way animals reproduce and performed the birth of life. Yes, as scripture states we are the workmanship of His hands, and He has provided us with gifts and talents to be able to live in the environment which He created for us here on earth.

> *Job 9:8-10 Easy-to-Read Version*
> ⁸ He alone made the skies,
>   and he walks on the ocean waves.
> ⁹ "God made the Bear, Orion, and the Pleiades.[a]
>   He made the planets that cross the southern sky.[b]
> ¹⁰ He does things too marvelous for people to understand.
>   He does too many miracles to count!
>   Footnotes
>   a. Job 9:9 Bear, Orion, and the Pleiades Names of well-known constellations (groups of stars) in the night sky.
>   b. Job 9:9 planets ... sky Literally, "Rooms of the South" or "Rooms of Teman." This might be the planets or the twelve constellations of the Zodiac. North of the equator, these seem to move across the southern sky.

Jesus demonstrates how He can empower us to help ourselves by living out the principles of God's righteousness while He is working to make these a permanent part of our spiritual makeup. We see many references to the heart of man in scripture. What Jesus is saying there are internal processes in man that determine how we choose to live our life. The Lord knows that man is self-centered which is a trait He placed in us. This is so we can learn what it takes for us to survive. He understands that without proper desires this trait leads to us establishing the wrong goals. That is why He says we need to learn to love ourselves. This is a process of understanding that it is more than just me in this life. It is a process of learning that we are essentially one creation comprised of many different individuals. We do not understand our interconnectivity and how God created us to function as one unit. We see this stated as being one with each other in scripture.

I am led to share an experience which the Lord provided for me. One night at prayer service after I had added my minor effort at stating a prayer. The Lord touched me in a special way. He initiated this by the sensation of a small warm spot implanted within me. It was like a finger from someone touching me within my body. Suddenly this warm spot began to expand and as it did, I became more and more in touch with the feeling of everything around me. This grew until I could feel the molecules around me and felt I was part of my environment (which is the whole universe). No this was not like the wind blowing on me. I began to be in touch with every aspect of my body down to the point I could even feel the hairs on my arms. Yes, I was one with His creation and an integral part of it. It was as though I was one with everything and it was part of me. The delight I felt is indescribable. I felt all within me was now complete. Then this stopped suddenly. I was afraid to share this at that time because I was unable to put it in a way that they could understand. My make up is that I am very shy and at the time I was not able to share the experience. I have since learned we are provided with these experiences not just for me alone, but they are provided to share these with others. Now I have learned that we need to share these spiritual experiences. The more I share this experience the more others confirm they too have had similar experiences. Now I believe that I would have missed an opportunity to gain even more if I had shared it at that time. This is a feeling I wish we can all experience and I know one day that will be the case.

This is why we should learn that every part of us is indeed a divine creation working together to makeup this wonderful body I was granted to have. Circumstances have been made for us to not appreciate it. We are influenced to use all manner of concoctions to help enhance us because we feel we are not acceptable the way we are. Jesus brings to us a different understanding.

Jesus has been appointed to help us to understand that God loves us enough to correct the ways of the world which rule our daily lives. Our lives are not the same as God originally designed us to be. So, Jesus has been designated by God Our Father to be our Savior. Jesus saves us from spiritual death at the end of this life. We are told Jesus is the way the truth and the life.

Ephesians 2:1-3 Easy-to-Read Version
From Death to Life
¹ In the past you were spiritually dead because of your sins and the things you did against God.
² Yes, in the past your lives were full of those sins. You lived the way the world lives, following the ruler of the evil powers[a] that are above the earth. That same spirit is now working in those who refuse to obey God.
³ In the past all of us lived like that, trying to please our sinful selves. We did all the things our bodies and minds wanted. Like everyone else in the world, we deserved to suffer God's anger just because of the way we were.
Footnotes
> a. *Ephesians 2:2 ruler of the evil powers See "Satan" in the Word List.*

Ephesians 4:26-28 Easy-to-Read Version
²⁶ "When you are angry, don't let that anger make you sin,"[a] and don't stay angry all day.
²⁷ Don't give the devil a way to defeat you.
²⁸ Whoever has been stealing must stop it and start working. They must use their hands for doing something good. Then they will have something to share with those who are poor.
Footnotes
> a. *Ephesians 4:26 Quote from Ps. 4:4 (Greek version).*

John 14:5-7 Easy-to-Read Version
⁵ Thomas said, "Lord, we don't know where you are going, so how can we know the way?"
⁶ Jesus answered, "I am the way, the truth, and the life. The only way to the Father is through me.
⁷ If you really knew me, you would know my Father too. But now you know the Father. You have seen him."

He is the way we can be fitted and transformed so we can have eternal life. He is the actualization of God's love toward us. Yes, Jesus is the physical and spiritual pathway to God and His works bring forgiveness because He has chosen to accept the punishment which we deserve for our sins satisfying God's justice. Jesus has taken on this for Himself. Now that does not mean that we are exempt from the punishment for our sins here on earth. What it does mean is that when God stands as judge to determine whether we deserve to have eternal life or eternal death. Jesus' sacrifice declares us not guilty. This is because we have repented and been transformed from following evil to being converted into encompassing righteousness. That is why we are told to confess our sins and to change our allegiance from one which follows Satan (the ways of the world, our selfish nature) to one who follows God's ways, to one which demonstrates Godly love.

Summary

Jesus is God's spokesperson or His designated chief commander or however you want to put it. Jesus has God's full authority. So, we need to pay attention to Jesus' instruction whether they be by spoken word direct from Him, or from his prophets, or those He has appointed to lead us into God's way of living and doing things in righteousness and Holiness, or through scripture. All these He uses to bring about our perfection orchestrated by His Holy Spirit. Each one of us plays an important part in this process. Scripture states Jesus' true followers know His voice. We cannot dismiss the fact that our perfection is Christ's work. We need to understand that anything less than perfection is unacceptable. The work Jesus performs must be perfect in God's sight or it is not complete. We are part of the whole and without each of us joined together in unity the work is incomplete. So, we need to accept that until all of us come to the point of being perfect in God's sight the work in us is not done or finished. Jesus stated on the cross "it is finished." What Jesus was saying is this step which is needed for our justification is done therefore the work of converting is us has begun. Perfection is not yet complete and will not be until everyone whose name which is written the book of life is included.

Jesus is God's commander in chief, His commandant, His chief representative, to bring us to where we need to be to meet His requirements for living with Him in heaven. Jesus is in charge of all of God's kingdom.

    a. We need to accept that Jesus provides us with the gift of eternal life which saves us from the eternal death which awaits those who do not accept His offer of salvation.

    b. We need to accept all our righteousness is provided through Jesus.

    c. Jesus will share powers from on High when we can be trusted to use them righteously under the guidance of the Holy Spirit learning the use of these as shown in scripture.

    d. Jesus will heal us physically and spiritually as the Father directs for the love which He has for us and our fellow saints and His entire creation.

    e. Jesus stands as our representative before God and the entire world and our defense against the devil and His sinful influence.

    f. It is through Jesus we are granted fellowship with Father God.

    g. Jesus is in control of all spiritual gifts and all angelic ministries.

    h. Jesus has been appointed by God to perform the task of providing the church which God wants to dwell with Him in heaven.

    i. We, those who have truly repented, are the church. The church is not a building, nor an institution, nor an organization. Jesus' true disciples are the church.

> ***Ephesians 3:9-11 Easy-to-Read Version***
> *⁹ And God gave me the work of telling all people about the plan for his secret truth. That secret truth has been hidden in him since the beginning of time. He is the one who created everything.*
> *¹⁰ His purpose was that all the rulers and powers in the heavenly places will now know the many different ways he shows his wisdom. They will know this because of the church.*

¹¹ This agrees with the plan God had since the beginning of time. He did what he planned, and he did it through Christ Jesus our Lord.

Hebrews 12:22-24 Easy-to-Read Version
²² But you have come to Mount Zion, to the city of the living God, the heavenly Jerusalem.[a] You have come to a place where thousands of angels have gathered to celebrate.
²³ You have come to the meeting of God's firstborn[b] children. Their names are written in heaven. You have come to God, the judge of all people. And you have come to the spirits of good people who have been made perfect.
²⁴ You have come to Jesus—the one who brought the new agreement from God to his people. You have come to the sprinkled blood[c] that tells us about better things than the blood of Abel.

Footnotes
- a. Hebrews 12:22 Jerusalem Here, the spiritual city of God's people.
- b. Hebrews 12:23 firstborn The first son born in a Jewish family had the most important place in the family and received special blessings. All of God's children are like that.
- c. Hebrews 12:24 sprinkled blood The blood (death) of Jesus.

Revelation 3:11-13 Easy-to-Read Version
¹¹ "I am coming soon. Hold on to the faith you have, so that no one can take away your crown.
¹² Those who win the victory will be pillars in the temple of my God. I will make that happen for them. They will never again have to leave God's temple. I will write on them the name of my God and the name of the city of my God. That city is the new Jerusalem.[a] It is coming down out of heaven from my God. I will also write my new name on them.
¹³ Everyone who hears this should listen to what the Spirit says to the churches.

Footnotes
- a. Revelation 3:12 new Jerusalem The spiritual city where God's people live with him.

b. God's glory is to bring about the salvation of His creation allowing them performing the purpose for which they were created.

Matthew 16:18 Amplified Bible

[18] And I say to you that you are [a]Peter, and on this [b]rock I will build My church; and the [c]gates of Hades (death) will not overpower it [by preventing the resurrection of the Christ].

Footnotes

a. Matthew 16:18 Gr petros, a small or detached stone.
b. Matthew 16:18 Gr petra, bedrock or a huge rock. Jesus uses a simple play on the Greek words petros and petra in this verse. Throughout the N.T. Christ is clearly depicted as both the foundation petra and chief cornerstone of the church. Here He praises Peter for his accurate confession of faith in Him as Messiah. Peter explains the role of believers as "living stones" in the church which is built on Christ as the foundation and cornerstone (1 Pet 2:5, 6).
c. Matthew 16:18 The physical death of Christ will not hinder the establishment of the church nor will death overtake the church.

CHAPTER 10

What lies before us?

EPHESIANS 4:23-25 EASY-TO-READ VERSION

²³ *You must be made new in your hearts and in your thinking.*
²⁴ *Be that new person who was made to be like God, truly good and pleasing to him.*
²⁵ *So you must stop telling lies. "You must always speak the truth to each other,"[a] because we all belong to each other in the same body.*
   Footnotes
   a)   Ephesians 4:25 Quote from Zech. 8:16.

ZECHARIAH 8:16 EASY-TO-READ VERSION

¹⁶ *But you must do this: Tell the truth to your neighbors. When you make decisions in your cities, be fair and do what is right. Do what brings peace.*

GENESIS 8:20-22 AMPLIFIED BIBLE

²⁰ *And Noah built an altar to the Lord, and took of every [ceremonially] clean animal and of every clean bird and offered burnt offerings on the altar.*
²¹ *The Lord smelled the pleasing aroma [a soothing, satisfying scent] and the Lord said to Himself, "I will never again curse the ground because of man, for the intent (strong inclination, desire) of man's heart is wicked from his youth; and I will never again destroy every living thing, as I have done.*
²² *"While the earth remains,*
   Seedtime and harvest,
   Cold and heat,
   Winter and summer,
   And day and night

Shall not cease."

We have to understand what God has planned for all creation. This has been explained by the concept of being one. All throughout the book of Ephesians and scripture the Lord emphasizes the fact that all things should be brought together as one. The concept of unity is expanded here to the nth degree. Look at these scriptures.

EPHESIANS 2:15-17 KING JAMES VERSION

15 Having abolished in his flesh the enmity, even the law of commandments contained in ordinances; for to make in himself of twain one new man, so making peace;
16 And that he might reconcile both unto God in one body by the cross, having slain the enmity thereby:
17 And came and preached peace to you which were afar off, and to them that were nigh.

EPHESIANS 2:15-17 AMPLIFIED BIBLE

15 by abolishing in His [own crucified] flesh the hostility caused by the Law with its commandments contained in ordinances [which He satisfied]; so that in Himself He might make the two into one new man, thereby establishing peace.
16 And [that He] might reconcile them both [Jew and Gentile, united] in one body to God through the cross, thereby putting to death the hostility.
17 And He came and preached the good news of peace to you [Gentiles] who were far away, and peace to those [Jews] who were near.

EPHESIANS 3:5-7 KING JAMES VERSION

5 Which in other ages was not made known unto the sons of men, as it is now revealed unto his holy apostles and prophets by the Spirit;
6 That the Gentiles should be fellowheirs, and of the same body, and partakers of his promise in Christ by the gospel:
7 Whereof I was made a minister, according to the gift of the grace of God given unto me by the effectual working of his power.

EPHESIANS 4:3-7 KING JAMES VERSION

3 Endeavouring to keep the unity of the Spirit in the bond of peace.

⁴ There is one body, and one Spirit, even as ye are called in one hope of your calling;
⁵ One Lord, one faith, one baptism,
⁶ One God and Father of all, who is above all, and through all, and in you all.
⁷ But unto every one of us is given grace according to the measure of the gift of Christ.

EPHESIANS 4:3-7 AMPLIFIED BIBLE

³ Make every effort to keep the oneness of the Spirit in the bond of peace [each individual working together to make the whole successful].
⁴ There is one body [of believers] and one Spirit—just as you were called to one hope when called [to salvation]—
⁵ one Lord, one faith, one baptism,
⁶ one God and Father of us all who is [sovereign] over all and [working] through all and [living] in all.
⁷ Yet grace [God's undeserved favor] was given to each one of us [not indiscriminately, but in different ways] in proportion to the measure of Christ's [rich and abundant] gift.

EPHESIANS 4:22-26 KING JAMES VERSION

²² That ye put off concerning the former conversation the old man, which is corrupt according to the deceitful lusts;
²³ And be renewed in the spirit of your mind;
²⁴ And that ye put on the new man, which after God is created in righteousness and true holiness.
²⁵ Wherefore putting away lying, speak every man truth with his neighbour: for we are members one of another.
²⁶ Be ye angry, and sin not: let not the sun go down upon your wrath:

EPHESIANS 4:22-26 AMPLIFIED BIBLE

²² that, regarding your previous way of life, you put off your old self [completely discard your former nature], which is being corrupted through deceitful desires,
²³ and be continually renewed in the spirit of your mind [having a fresh, untarnished mental and spiritual attitude],
²⁴ and put on the new self [the regenerated and renewed nature], created in God's image, [godlike] in the righteousness and holiness of the truth [living in a way that expresses to God your gratitude for your salvation].

²⁵ Therefore, rejecting all falsehood [whether lying, defrauding, telling half-truths, spreading rumors, any such as these], speak truth each one with his neighbor, for we are all parts of one another [and we are all parts of the body of Christ].

²⁶ Be angry [at sin—at immorality, at injustice, at ungodly behavior], yet do not sin; do not let your anger [cause you shame, nor allow it to] last until the sun goes down.

EPHESIANS 5:28-32 KING JAMES VERSION

²⁸ So ought men to love their wives as their own bodies. He that loveth his wife loveth himself.

²⁹ For no man ever yet hated his own flesh; but nourisheth and cherisheth it, even as the Lord the church:

³⁰ For we are members of his body, of his flesh, and of his bones.

³¹ For this cause shall a man leave his father and mother, and shall ᵇᵉ joined unto his wife, and they two shall be one flesh.

³² This is a great mystery: but I speak concerning Christ and the church.

EPHESIANS 5:28-32 AMPLIFIED BIBLE

²⁸ Even so husbands should and are morally obligated to love their own wives as [being in a sense] their own bodies. He who loves his own wife loves himself.

²⁹ For no one ever hated his own body, but [instead] he nourishes and protects and cherishes it, just as Christ does the church, 30 because we are members (parts) of His body.

³¹ For this reason a man shall leave his father and his mother and shall be joined [and be faithfully devoted] to his wife, and the two shall become [a]one flesh.

³² This mystery [of two becoming one] is great; but I am speaking with reference to [the relationship of] Christ and the church.

Footnotes

a) Ephesians 5:31 The bond between husband and wife supersedes all other relationships.

Are we so blind that we cannot see the importance of us becoming united (being one). The Lord sees this as an absolute. Here we can see that the object of our conversion is to make us one with God, Jesus and the Holy Spirit and one another. This is so that God's plan to have us all be in His presence at the end may be fulfilled. This does not mean we lose our individuality, but it means we gain things which we cannot otherwise accomplish. Examine what these scriptures are saying and not just these but many more. First it states that we are all one body of believers not just Baptist, or Catholic, or Evangelicals, or any other titled religion but one body of believers in Christ Jesus. So where do denominations come in? They do not. It goes on to say we are one hope one baptism, with one Spirit, one God one Savoir. So why are so many churches claiming to be the only way? Jesus is the only way. It even says in this revelation provided to us through Paul there is no Jew or gentile in Christ. We are even told elsewhere in scripture in Christ there is not either male or female, nationality, or tribes. There are no things which separate us into groups other than the fact some have distinct roles which they are called to fulfill. None is greater nor is any less. We are all the same in Him as far as His salvation goes. See how this is stated in the letter to the Galatians.

GALATIANS 3:27-29 KING JAMES VERSION

27 For as many of you as have been baptized into Christ have put on Christ.
28 There is neither Jew nor Greek, there is neither bond nor free, there is neither male nor female: for ye are all one in Christ Jesus.
29 And if ye be Christ's, then are ye Abraham's seed, and heirs according to the promise.

Christ is building one church not a bunch of little ones but one only. There is no room for division, just diversity in the way we were created and the source of our calling. Note that neither skin color, nor nationality, nor any other way we try to describe who we are matters. We are all included in one salvation which is God's gift of eternal life. Look at Jesus's disciples and how they argued about being the next in charge.

LUKE 22:19-29 EASY-TO-READ VERSION

19 Then he took some bread and thanked God for it. He broke off some pieces, gave them to the apostles and said, "This bread is my body that I am giving for you. Eat this to remember me."
20 In the same way, after supper, Jesus took the cup of wine and said, "This wine represents the new agreement from God to his people. It will begin when my blood is poured out for you."[a]
Who Will Turn Against Jesus?

> ²¹ *Jesus said, "But here on this table is the hand of the one who will hand me over to my enemies.*
> ²² *The Son of Man will do what God has planned. But it will be very bad for the one who hands over the Son of Man to be killed."*
> ²³ *Then the apostles asked each other, "Which one of us would do that?"*
> Be Like a Servant
> ²⁴ *Later, the apostles began to argue about which one of them was the most important.*
> ²⁵ *But Jesus said to them, "The kings of the world rule over their people, and those who have authority over others want to be called 'the great providers for the people.'*
> ²⁶ *But you must not be like that. The one with the most authority among you should act as if he is the least important. The one who leads should be like one who serves.*
> ²⁷ *Who is more important: the one serving or the one sitting at the table being served? Everyone thinks it's the one being served, right? But I have been with you as the one who serves.*
> ²⁸ *"You men have stayed with me through many struggles. 29 So I give you authority to rule with me in the kingdom the Father has given me.*
> Footnotes
> a. Luke 22:20 A few Greek copies do not have Jesus' words in the last part of verse 19 and all of verse 20.

Do we hear similar arguments in industry today? Does not the CEOs of most businesses state that they are the most important part of the firm and without them the company will fail. These CEOs claim that is why they deserve such high pay.

The disciples were controlled by their human nature, reasoning that dictated that they should receive special recognition or authority. Our specialness comes because of who we are in Christ Jesus. This is being one and loved by Him and Father God. We should be happy to be saved but so much of the selfish nature calls out for us to be above everyone else.

We hear so much rhetoric which teaches division in the so-called church today. The call from Jesus is to have one faith one baptism and one hope all accomplished by one Spirit which is the Holy Spirit of the Lord which is given to all true believers. Jesus told us as an example not everyone who calls himself is a Jew is a true Jew, but only one who is Jew in his heart is the one who is true. It is not a name which defines the internal man.

EPHESIANS 2:1-10 KING JAMES VERSION

¹ And you hath he quickened, who were dead in trespasses and sins;
² Wherein in time past ye walked according to the course of this world, according to the prince of the power of the air, the spirit that now worketh in the children of disobedience:
³ Among whom also we all had our conversation in times past in the lusts of our flesh, fulfilling the desires of the flesh and of the mind; and were by nature the children of wrath, even as others.
⁴ But God, who is rich in mercy, for his great love wherewith he loved us,
⁵ Even when we were dead in sins, hath quickened us together with Christ, (by grace ye are saved;)
⁶ And hath raised us up together, and made us sit together in heavenly places in Christ Jesus:
⁷ That in the ages to come he might shew the exceeding riches of his grace in his kindness toward us through Christ Jesus.
⁸ For by grace are ye saved through faith; and that not of yourselves: it is the gift of God:
⁹ Not of works, lest any man should boast.
¹⁰ For we are his workmanship, created in Christ Jesus unto good works, which God hath before ordained that we should walk in them.

Since in Christ there is no separation between Jew and Gentile, we are one in Him and only those who are one in their heart are His.

PSALM 24:3-5 KING JAMES VERSION

³ Who shall ascend into the hill of the Lord? or who shall stand in his holy place?
⁴ He that hath clean hands, and a pure heart; who hath not lifted up his soul unto vanity, nor sworn deceitfully.
⁵ He shall receive the blessing from the Lord, and righteousness from the God of his salvation.

ROMANS 2:28-29 KING JAMES VERSION

²⁸ For he is not a Jew, which is one outwardly; neither is that circumcision, which is outward in the flesh:

²⁹ But he is a Jew, which is one inwardly; and circumcision is that of the heart, in the spirit, and not in the letter; whose praise is not of men, but of God.

It is the inner transformation which occurs inside us through the work of the Holy Spirit not what we claim that makes us a true believer. It is not just by calling ourselves a Christian which makes us a true one. It only occurs through this transformation which comes as the result of the work of Jesus that we become true Christians. It is not through our human effort.

MARK 7:21-23 KING JAMES VERSION

²¹ For from within, out of the heart of men, proceed evil thoughts, adulteries, fornications, murders,
²² Thefts, covetousness, wickedness, deceit, lasciviousness, an evil eye, blasphemy, pride, foolishness:
²³ All these evil things come from within, and defile the man.

EPHESIANS 2:8-10 KING JAMES VERSION

⁸ For by grace are ye saved through faith; and that not of yourselves: it is the gift of God:
⁹ Not of works, lest any man should boast.
¹⁰ For we are his workmanship, created in Christ Jesus unto good works, which God hath before ordained that we should walk in them.

So, it is not what name we use but by but by the work of Christ in us which identifies what a true believer or Christian is. It is faith which calls us to practice unity in Christ Jesus. So, if you are truly baptized then you are on the road to salvation and eternal life. This requires a reorientation of our beliefs which determines how we live. When we turn from the ways of the world which calls us to place ourselves first, then true transformed living begins. Transformation is evidenced by our adopting new habit patterns which are based on the same love which God has for us. This love is not selfish. It is one which considers every part of God's creation as being just as important if not more important than ourselves. This means that I start to understand and desire to act the same as God does. I begin to see the injustice created in the worldly way we formerly chose to live which has been influenced by the evil one. We reject this behavior and start practicing the new inner work which God places in us. In Him we can resist sinful lusts of the flesh and start working from within which produces righteous works of conduct toward each other. Paul is led in all the New Testament to emphasize that we become one in all things spiritual and physical. Remember how Paul describes the church as a single organism (our body) with many parts that all work together for the good of the whole.

ROMANS 7:3-5 EASY-TO-READ VERSION

3 But if she marries another man while her husband is still alive, the law says she is guilty of adultery. But if her husband dies, she is made free from the law of marriage. So if she marries another man after her husband dies, she is not guilty of adultery.
4 In the same way, my brothers and sisters, your old selves died and you became free from the law through the body of Christ. Now you belong to someone else. You belong to the one who was raised from death. We belong to Christ so that we can be used in service to God.
5 In the past we were ruled by our sinful selves. The law made us want to do sinful things. And those sinful desires controlled our bodies, so that what we did only brought us spiritual death.

ROMANS 12:4-6 EASY-TO-READ VERSION

4 Each one of us has one body, and that body has many parts. These parts don't all do the same thing.
5 In the same way, we are many people, but in Christ we are all one body. We are the parts of that body, and each part belongs to all the others.
6 We all have different gifts. Each gift came because of the grace God gave us. Whoever has the gift of prophecy should use that gift in a way that fits the kind of faith they have.

See here oneness is exemplified. Not the distorted attempts which are human initated, but the one which God created from the beginning. You see all we do is to be based on doing what is best for us all not just a single individual. Then everyone will receive what they need because God planned for it to be this way.

MATTHEW 5:44-46 KING JAMES VERSION

44 But I say unto you, Love your enemies, bless them that curse you, do good to them that hate you, and pray for them which despitefully use you, and persecute you;

⁴⁵ That ye may be the children of your Father which is in heaven: for he maketh his sun to rise on the evil and on the good, and sendeth rain on the just and on the unjust.

⁴⁶ For if ye love them which love you, what reward have ye? do not even the publicans the same?

LUKE 13:1-3 EASY-TO-READ VERSION

Change Your Hearts
¹ Some people there with Jesus at that time told him about what had happened to some worshipers from Galilee. Pilate had them killed. Their blood was mixed with the blood of the animals they had brought for sacrificing.
² Jesus answered, "Do you think this happened to those people because they were more sinful than all other people from Galilee?
³ No, they were not. But if you don't decide now to change your lives, you will all be destroyed like those people!

Scripture tells us the Lord causes rain to fall on the just and unjust just alike. Not because the Lord loves one more than another but because He wants us to understand that He loves all His creation, and he wants good for all of it not just for some parts. So, we should see that none of us should suffer in this life if we can help it. As it says in scripture, if one part of the body suffers, we all suffer.

1 CORINTHIANS 12:25-27 EASY-TO-READ VERSION

²⁵ God did this so that our body would not be divided. God wanted the different parts to care the same for each other.
²⁶ If one part of the body suffers, then all the other parts suffer with it. Or if one part is honored, then all the other parts share its honor.
²⁷ All of you together are the body of Christ. Each one of you is a part of that body.

Oneness is about the way we treat and accept one another. It is more than thinking the same, it is the consideration which we have for each other so that no one is impoverished or mistreated. Therefore, we cannot and will not stand for our brothers and sisters living a life which is any less than that God desires for each of us.

God created Adam and Eve in a garden with all they needed for life, yet they allowed the influence of Satan to separate them from paradise to a life of misery and suffering; just as we have. Oneness calls us to eliminate all misery and suffering so that none lacks, and no one is mistreated. God is working to redefine what our life on earth is like. We are to allow God to transform life on earth to be the same as it is in heaven. God is transforming believers so that He can do away with pain and suffering on earth just as it is in heaven. This includes us treating each other with true loving kindness and honesty. We are to build up and tear down but that requires a change within. It should be stated this way. Learning a new way of treating others and ourself by practicing the same love as God has for us. All of which initiates from within.

JEREMIAH 1:5-10 EASY-TO-READ VERSION

⁵ "Before I made you in your mother's womb,
I knew you.
Before you were born,
I chose you for a special work.
I chose you to be a prophet to the nations."
⁶ Then I said, "But, Lord God, I don't know how to speak. I am only a boy."
⁷ But the Lord said to me,
"Don't say, 'I am only a boy.'
You must go everywhere I send you
and say everything I tell you to say.
⁸ Don't be afraid of anyone.
I am with you, and I will protect you."
This message is from the Lord.
⁹ Then the Lord reached out with his hand and touched my mouth.
He said to me,
"Jeremiah, I am putting my words in your mouth.
¹⁰ Today I have put you in charge of nations and kingdoms.
You will pull up and tear down.
You will destroy and overthrow.
You will build up and plant."

JEREMIAH 24:5-7 EASY-TO-READ VERSION

⁵ The Lord, the God of Israel, said, "The people of Judah were taken from their country. Their enemy brought them to Babylon. Those people will be like these good figs. I will be kind to them.

⁶ *I will protect them. I will bring them back to the land of Judah. I will not tear them down—I will build them up. I will not pull them up—I will plant them so that they can grow.*
⁷ *I will make them want to know me. They will know that I am the Lord. They will be my people, and I will be their God. I will do this because the prisoners in Babylon will turn to me with their whole hearts."*

JUDE 19-21 EASY-TO-READ VERSION

¹⁹ *These are the people who divide you. They are not spiritual, because they don't have the Spirit.*
²⁰ *But you, dear friends, use your most holy faith to build yourselves up even stronger. Pray with the help of the Holy Spirit.*
²¹ *Keep yourselves safe in God's love, as you wait for the Lord Jesus Christ in his mercy to give you eternal life.*

1 THESSALONIANS 5:10-12 AMPLIFIED BIBLE

¹⁰ *who died [willingly] for us, so that whether we are awake (alive) or asleep (dead) [at Christ's appearing], we will live together with Him [sharing eternal life].*
¹¹ *Therefore encourage and comfort one another and build up one another, just as you are doing.*
Christian Conduct
¹² *Now we ask you, brothers and sisters, to appreciate those who diligently work among you [recognize, acknowledge, and respect your leaders], who are in charge over you in the Lord and who give you instruction,*

We can see it is about what we believe and whom we choose to be and obey. It is not just about a doctrine or creed or some other philosophy. It is about being transformed so that we no longer resemble the earthly but the heavenly. Just as it says in scripture, I do not know what will happen, but I know when Jesus appears I will know Him because I will be like Him. If you see this as something bad, then you are following the evil one not the Lord.

LUKE 12:35-37 EASY-TO-READ VERSION

Always Be Ready
³⁵ *"Be ready! Be fully dressed and have your lights shining.*
³⁶ *Be like servants who are waiting for their master to come home from a wedding party. The master comes and knocks, and the servants immediately open the door for him.*

³⁷ When their master sees that they are ready and waiting for him, it will be a great day for those servants. I can tell you without a doubt, the master will get himself ready to serve a meal and tell the servants to sit down. Then he will serve them.

ROMANS 6:4-8 EASY-TO-READ VERSION

⁴ So when we were baptized, we were buried with Christ and took part in his death. And just as Christ was raised from death by the wonderful power of the Father, so we can now live a new life.
⁵ Christ died, and we have been joined with him by dying too. So we will also be joined with him by rising from death as he did.
⁶ We know that our old life was put to death on the cross with Christ. This happened so that our sinful selves would have no power over us. Then we would not be slaves to sin.
⁷ Anyone who has died is made free from sin's control.
⁸ If we died with Christ, we know that we will also live with him.

2 CORINTHIANS 13:3-8 EASY-TO-READ VERSION

³ You want proof that Christ is speaking through me. My proof is that he is not weak in dealing with you but is showing his power among you.
⁴ It is true that Christ was weak when he was killed on the cross, but he lives now by God's power. It is also true that we share his weakness, but in dealing with you, we will be alive in him by God's power.
⁵ Look closely at yourselves. Test yourselves to see if you are living in the faith. Don't you realize that Christ Jesus is in you? Of course, if you fail the test, he is not in you.
⁶ But I hope you will see that we have not failed the test.
⁷ We pray to God that you will not do anything wrong. Our concern here is not for people to see that we have passed the test in our work with you. Our main concern is that you do what is right, even if it looks as if we have failed the test.
⁸ We cannot do anything that is against the truth but only what promotes the truth.

PHILIPPIANS 3:18-21 EASY-TO-READ VERSION

¹⁸ There are many who live like enemies of the cross of Christ. I have often told you about them. And it makes me cry to tell you about them now.
¹⁹ The way they live is leading them to destruction. They have replaced God with their own desires. They do shameful things,

> *and they are proud of what they do. They think only about earthly things.*
> *[20] But the government that rules us is in heaven. We are waiting for our Savior, the Lord Jesus Christ, to come from there.*
> *[21] He will change our humble bodies and make them like his own glorious body. Christ can do this by his power, with which he is able to rule everything.* 1 John 3:1-3
>
> **EASY-TO-READ VERSION WE ARE GOD'S CHILDREN**
>
> *[1] The Father has loved us so much! This shows how much he loved us: We are called children of God. And we really are his children. But the people in the world don't understand that we are God's children, because they have not known him.*
> *[2] Dear friends, now we are children of God. We have not yet been shown what we will be in the future. But we know that when Christ comes again, we will be like him. We will see him just as he is.*
> *[3] He is pure, and everyone who has this hope in him keeps themselves pure like Christ.*

Oneness is a change in our inner man to the point the outward man and the one inside display God in us. There is only one gospel, and it is not what most of us practice. That is why Jesus says be ye perfect as your Father in heaven is perfect. Yes, oneness has to do with us being made perfect and all that we are and all that we do will be lived in this way.

Summary

We are being shaped into the image of God if we allow it. This is one that is based on pure love, pure thoughts, and pure living for all of us not just me. If we are working for anything else, we are missing the point. Without the Holy Spirit we can easily be shifted off course and end up doing the wrong thing or following the wrong set of teachings. Are we truly seeking His kingdom and His righteousness or are we aimlessly being tossed back and forth by every whim of doctrine? Remember Jesus' teaching is not doctrine but the freedom to live life as God designed not tainted by the evil one. So, our call to oneness initiates from above and is completed from within by the Lord through the Holy Spirit.

Our perfection and completion and oneness are through the work of Jesus which sets us free from the works of darkness or the works of the world into works of light and purity.

EPHESIANS 2:15-17 KING JAMES VERSION

15 Having abolished in his flesh the enmity, even the law of commandments contained in ordinances; for to make in himself of twain one new man, so making peace;

16 And that he might reconcile both unto God in one body by the cross, having slain the enmity thereby:

17 And came and preached peace to you which were afar off, and to them that were nigh.

EPHESIANS 2:15-17 AMPLIFIED BIBLE

15 by abolishing in His [own crucified] flesh the hostility caused by the Law with its commandments contained in ordinances [which He satisfied]; so that in Himself He might make the two into one new man, thereby establishing peace.

16 And [that He] might reconcile them both [Jew and Gentile, united] in one body to God through the cross, thereby putting to death the hostility.

17 And He came and preached the good news of peace to you [Gentiles] who were far away, and peace to those [Jews] who were near.

COLOSSIANS 1:13-14 KING JAMES VERSION

13 Who hath delivered us from the power of darkness, and hath translated us into the kingdom of his dear Son:

14 In whom we have redemption through his blood, even the forgiveness of sins:

Whether we know it or not we are all eternal beings. We who believe are destined for eternal life rather than eternal death. Eternal death is the result of refusing the Lord's offer of God's everlasting love and His compassionate nature. Without Jesus and His loving ways humanity is destined for eternal death. Many do not understand that God groups us into two portions. One is those who have accepted the offer of forgiveness after acceptance of Jesus and our commitment to repent. This then prepares us for the work of

Jesus and the Holy spirit which transforms us into a state acceptable to God. The other portion is eternal death which is reserved for those who refuse to repent and want to deny Christ Jesus.

HEBREWS 11:30-40 KING JAMES VERSION

30 By faith the walls of Jericho fell down, after they were compassed about seven days.

31 By faith the harlot Rahab perished not with them that believed not, when she had received the spies with peace.

32 And what shall I more say? for the time would fail me to tell of Gedeon, and of Barak, and of Samson, and of Jephthae; of David also, and Samuel, and of the prophets:

33 Who through faith subdued kingdoms, wrought righteousness, obtained promises, stopped the mouths of lions.

34 Quenched the violence of fire, escaped the edge of the sword, out of weakness were made strong, waxed valiant in fight, turned to flight the armies of the aliens.

35 Women received their dead raised to life again: and others were tortured, not accepting deliverance; that they might obtain a better resurrection:

36 And others had trial of cruel mockings and scourgings, yea, moreover of bonds and imprisonment:

37 They were stoned, they were sawn asunder, were tempted, were slain with the sword: they wandered about in sheepskins and goatskins; being destitute, afflicted, tormented;

38 (Of whom the world was not worthy:) they wandered in deserts, and in mountains, and in dens and caves of the earth.

39 And these all, having obtained a good report through faith, received not the promise:

40 God having provided some better thing for us, that they without us should not be made perfect.

1 PETER 2:9-13 AMPLIFIED BIBLE

9 But you are a chosen race, a royal priesthood, a consecrated nation, a [special] people for God's own possession, so that you may proclaim the excellencies [the wonderful deeds and virtues and perfections] of Him who called you out of darkness into His marvelous light.

10 Once you were not a people [at all], but now you are God's people; once you had not received mercy, but now you have received mercy.

¹¹ *Beloved, I urge you as aliens and strangers [in this world] to abstain from the sensual urges [those dishonorable desires] that wage war against the soul.*
¹² *Keep your behavior excellent among the [unsaved] Gentiles [conduct yourself honorably, with graciousness and integrity], so that [a]for whatever reason they may slander you as evildoers, yet by observing your good deeds they may [instead come to] glorify God [b]in the day of visitation [when He looks upon them with mercy].*
Honor Authority
¹³ *Submit yourselves to [the authority of] every human institution for the sake of the Lord [to honor His name], whether it is to a king as one in a position of power,*

Footnotes
a) 1 Peter 2:12 Lit in that which.
b) 1 Peter 2:12 Another view interprets this as the day when the wicked are judged by God.

1 JOHN 3:1-10 KING JAMES VERSION

¹ *Behold, what manner of love the Father hath bestowed upon us, that we should be called the sons of God: therefore the world knoweth us not, because it knew him not.*
² *Beloved, now are we the sons of God, and it doth not yet appear what we shall be: but we know that, when he shall appear, we shall be like him; for we shall see him as he is.*
³ *And every man that hath this hope in him purifieth himself, even as he is pure.*
⁴ *Whosoever committeth sin transgresseth also the law: for sin is the transgression of the law.*
⁵ *And ye know that he was manifested to take away our sins; and in him is no sin.*
⁶ *Whosoever abideth in him sinneth not: whosoever sinneth hath not seen him, neither known him.*
⁷ *Little children, let no man deceive you: he that doeth righteousness is righteous, even as he is righteous.*
⁸ *He that committeth sin is of the devil; for the devil sinneth from the beginning. For this purpose the Son of God was manifested, that he might destroy the works of the devil.*
⁹ *Whosoever is born of God doth not commit sin; for his seed remaineth in him: and he cannot sin, because he is born of God.*

¹⁰ *In this the children of God are manifest, and the children of the devil: whosoever doeth not righteousness is not of God, neither he that loveth not his brother.*

1 JOHN 5:11-12 REVISED STANDARD VERSION

¹¹ *And this is the testimony, that God gave us eternal life, and this life is in his Son.*
¹² *He who has the Son has life; he who has not the Son of God has not life.*

These words I am led to leave with you.

Do All Things as Unto The Lord With Joy And Gladness

Postscript

I would like to ask a favor of you. I would appreciate it if you would provide an honest evaluation of this book and post it on my Facebook page for this book and if you have an Amzon.com account please add it there also. If you wish I would also like your permission to share your comments with others.

Appendix

Index

accept, 8, 14, 16, 31, 33, 44, 45, 48, 49, 50, 51, 56, 61, 78, 82, 84, 101, 102, 111, 135, 168
afford, 77
agreement, 49
apostle, **V**, **1**, **2**, **4**, **48**
appearance, 84, 88
appointee, **3**
baptized, 29, 47, 69, 75, 81, 82, 163, 166
battle, 58, 84, 97, 98, 100, 103, 110
behavior, 15, 32, 56, 63, 89, 90, 91, 94, 95, 99, 162
behaviors, 63, 102
<u>believe</u>, 2, 28, 41, 53, 54, 61, 84, 170
believers, 2, 18, 28, 41, 46, 56, 90, 92, 94, 96, 103, 161, 163, 164
blame, 12, 39
blessings, 11, 16, 42
blind, 52, 53, 61, 74, 162
boast, 30, 49, 51, 165, 166
brothers, 18, 30, 37, 41, 70, 109, 168
called, 4, 19, 28, 37, 47, 52, 53, 63, 70, 80, 81, 83, 84, 92, 96, 161, 163, 166, 168, 175, 189
candlesticks, 27, 29
change, 30, 44, 46, 48, 52, 66, 69, 75, 80, 88, 102, 113, 169, 172
choice, 2, 8, 13, 14, 16, 31, 45, 84

choose, 7, 12, 15, 44, 58, 74, 77, 87, 98, 101, 166, 170
Christ, IV, V, 1, 2, 3, 9, 11, 12, 17, 18, 19, 20, 29, 30, 31, 32, 33, 36, 37, 39, 40, 41, 44, 51, 53, 54, 55, 61, 62, 63, 64, 68, 69, 70, 71, 73, 75, 80, 81, 83, 88, 89, 90, 91, 93, 94, 95, 103, 109, 113, 160, 161, 162, 163, 165, 166, 173, 188, 190
Christian, 31, 33, 40, 49, 65, 79, 89, 103, 132
Christians, 30, 33, 69, 132, 134, 135
commandments, 74, 75, 160, 173
commitment, 33, 102, 173, 189
conditional, 54
conditions, 12, 43, 45, 54, 134
conduct, 16, 45, 54, 56, 63, 75, 98, 105, 112, 166
conscience, 14, 16, 17, 18, 19, 20, 58, 86
conversion, 48, 64, 162
converted, 36, 37, 135
convinced, 48
creation, 8, 12, 30, 88, 102, 111, 160, 166
death, 6, 19, 30, 45, 54, 55, 73, 74, 75, 81, 87, 88, 99, 100, 101, 132, 160, 173
desire, 30, 40, 45, 64, 66, 76, 94, 98, 99, 132, 166
destiny, 33, 77
devil, 6, 30, 32, 35, 36, 50, 57, 77, 82, 84, 89, 96, 101, 108,

109, 117, 120, 127, 133, 134, 135, 140, 154, 156, 175
difference, 36, 70, 75, 80, 84, 88
disciple, 53, 87
disobedient, 19, 58, 60
divine, **3**, **4**, **12**, **19**, **27**, **34**, **78**
divinity, 14
doctrines, 36, 103
dominion, 77
duty, 8, 65, 80
ears to hear, 5, 31, 37
educated, 60
ego, 87
Enoch, **8**
Ephesus, **V**, **1**, **2**, **8**, **27**, **28**, **34**, **43**, **51**
equal, 33
eternal life, 29, 36, 37, 69, 70, 75, 101, 102, 132, 134, 163, 166, 173, 176
evil, 27, 35, 36, 44, 50, 51, 54, 55, 56, 61, 62, 63, 69, 73, 78, 82, 88, 91, 95, 96, 97, 98, 100, 101, 110, 120, 166, 170
evil powers, 55, 56, 60, 73, 88, 148, 154
faith, 40, 44, 48, 49, 74, 78, 80, 84, 90, 94, 97, 101, 102, 111, 121, 161, 164, 165, 166, 174
faithful, V, 1, 2, 6, 8, 132, 133
Father, 3, 8, 9, 11, 35, 43, 49, 63, 74, 76, 80, 87, 88, 91, 94, 95, 99, 100, 161, 172, 175

flesh, 3, 17, 18, 19, 51, 60, 76, 78, 96, 98, 100, 101, 111, 120, 160, 162, 165, 166, 173
fooled, 62, 77, 87, 88
forever, 7, 15, 76
free, 43, 45, 51, 56, 78, 102, 163, 172
freedom, 12, 54, 172
gift, 18, 29, 30, 33, 37, 48, 49, 54, 55, 56, 69, 73, 78, 82, 88, 93, 102, 160, 161, 165, 166
gifts, 7, 11, 35, 61
glory, 12, 31, 39, 70, 80, 94, 100, 132, 134
God's will, 6, 109
godly, 18, 80, 86, 91, 95
good time, 58
grace, 12, 14, 18, 30, 39, 40, 41, 42, 43, 44, 45, 48, 49, 50, 51, 54, 55, 56, 71, 73, 80, 88, 93, 160, 161, 165, 166, 190
Grace, III, 9, 14, 39, 42, 43, 190
guides, 54
heavenly, 11, 30, 40, 41, 54, 55, 73, 88, 93, 96, 115, 165, 170
Holy, 6, 8, 12, 15, 16, 17, 18, 28, 29, 30, 32, 33, 35, 36, 40, 41, 42, 43, 45, 47, 49, 54, 60, 64, 65, 66, 69, 74, 82, 86, 88, 90, 91, 92, 95, 96, 98, 99, 101, 103, 108, 163, 164, 166, 172, 173, 189
Holy Ghost, 17, 29, 30, 82

Holy Spirit, 6, 16, 18, 28, 30, 32, 33, 35, 36, 40, 41, 45, 47, 49, 54, 60, 64, 65, 66, 69, 74, 87, 88, 90, 92, 96, 98, 99, 101, 102, 103, 108, 163, 164, 166, 172, 189
human, 3, 12, 18, 34, 43, 56, 114
Idol worship, 67
Imitators, 90, 94
immorality, 32, 67, 89, 90, 94, 162
inner person, 88
inner self, 69
life everlasting, 27
light and truth, 84
limitations, 11
Lord, **IV, 3, 4, 5, 7, 8, 9, 11, 12, 27, 28, 29, 31, 34, 36, 40, 41, 46, 47, 48, 49, 50, 51, 54, 56, 58, 61, 62, 63, 70, 75, 82, 83, 84, 89, 91, 93, 94, 95, 96, 98, 99, 100, 101, 102, 103, 108, 111, 120, 133, 160, 161, 162, 164, 165, 170, 172**
Lord Jesus, **3, 8, 9, 11, 29, 40, 41, 47, 63, 82, 91, 94, 95**
love, 3, 8, 12, 27, 28, 30, 33, 35, 36, 37, 39, 40, 42, 43, 44, 52, 54, 61, 62, 63, 66, 70, 76, 80, 88, 90, 94, 106, 132, 135, 162, 165, 166, 169, 172, 173, 175
lust, 75, 76, 99
lustful desires, 80
ministers, 3, 37
mislead, 60

moral, 20, 31, 75, 89, 90, 91, 94, 95, 97, 114
old way of life, 67, 69
Pamper, 77
patience, 27, 33, 74, 120
Paul, 1, 2, 3, 4, 8, 28, 48, 49, 50, 92, 96, 98, 100, 105
Pentecost, 80, 132
perfection, 16, 44, 49, 61, 98, 172
performance, 75
perish, 18, 45, 82, 87
permission, II, 45, 69, 98, 177
physical, 82, 92, 96, 98, 100, 103
praise, 12, 39, 53, 80, 91, 95, 165
predestined, 13, 16
preordained, 14, 43
presence, 12, 14, 16, 31, 33, 45, 49, 51, 84, 89, 92, 96, 98, 163
Prince of the power of the air, 56
prophecy, 3, 6, 29, 36, 37, 63, 78, 83, 132, 134
prophets, 35, 37, 61, 93, 103, 160, 174
pure, 18, 41, 80, 165, 172, 175
quickened, 40, 165
real, 4, 61, 82, 103
redemption, 16, 19, 32, 39, 90, 173
regenerates, 69
religion, 70, 75, 103
repent, 27, 36, 37, 45, 48, 74, 101, 114, 134, 173
repents, 50, 101

reside, 11, 15, 98
resist, 45, 77, 96, 101, 108, 166
righteous, 15, 33, 37, 42, 45, 102, 106, 113, 166, 175
rules, 19, 43
sacrifice, 30, 34, 62, 80, 90, 94
salvation, 32, 39, 43, 48, 50, 51, 71, 80, 88, 89, 91, 95, 97, 101, 103, 120, 121, 134, 161, 162, 163, 165, 166
satin, 56, 60, 65, 78, 86, 98, 100, 103, 108, 115, 168
selfish, III, 73, 86, 98, 164, 166
selfishness, 60, 78
sermons, 79
serve, 7, 8, 19, 67, 189
sin, III, 18, 30, 32, 33, 37, 40, 43, 45, 50, 52, 56, 63, 67, 73, 76, 89, 90, 91, 95, 99, 101, 102, 161, 162, 175
sinful, 33, 35, 45, 49, 54, 55, 56, 60, 63, 69, 73, 88, 98, 102, 105, 112, 166
sisters, 18, 30, 37, 109, 168
social, 67, 70, 75
Son of God, 3, 47, 54, 61, 74, 175, 176
spiritual, 11, 18, 31, 32, 35, 63, 66, 82, 87, 89, 91, 95, 96, 97, 98, 100, 101, 105, 120, 161
Spiritual, 16
spoil, 58
surrender, 80
surrendering, 75
terms, 14, 44
transforming, 40, 45, 75, 88

understanding, 6, 18, 31, 32, 33, 36, 37, 50, 61, 63, 69, 74, 75, 77, 89, 90, 98, 104
valueless, 87
very obvious, 75
wealth, 33, 75, 77
will of God, V, 1, 2, 6, 8, 76, 80
willingness, 64
wisdom, 11, 18, 39, 50, 91, 93, 95, 134
works, 3, 4, 19, 27, 30, 35, 36, 37, 40, 45, 49, 52, 54, 56, 62, 63, 66, 70, 71, 74, 75, 81, 86, 100, 103, 109, 120, 165, 166, 172, 175, 189, 190
world, 3, 12, 18, 34, 39, 44, 52, 53, 55, 56, 58, 60, 66, 73, 74, 76, 78, 80, 84, 88, 93, 94, 96, 99, 100, 101, 102, 108, 117, 120, 165, 166, 172, 174, 175

Scripture References

COPYRIGHT   II
TABLE OF CONTENTS   III
    EPHESIANS 1:1 KING JAMES VERSION   V
    EPHESIANS 4:1-15 KING JAMES VERSION   V
    1 JOHN 3:18 KING JAMES VERSION   V
    1 JOHN 3:18 EASY-TO-READ VERSION   VI
PAUL'S HEAVENLY CREDENTIALS   1
    EPHESIANS 1:1 KING JAMES VERSION   1
    EPHESIANS 4:1-15 KING JAMES VERSION   1
    EPHESIANS 1:1 AMPLIFIED BIBLE   2
    REVELATION 1:1-3 NEW INTERNATIONAL VERSION   3
    DEUTERONOMY 29:3-5 NEW INTERNATIONAL VERSION   4
    JEREMIAH 6:9-11 KING JAMES VERSION   4
    EZEKIEL 12:1-3 NEW INTERNATIONAL VERSION   5
    MARK 4:22-24 NEW INTERNATIONAL VERSION   5
    MARK 4:1-10 NEW INTERNATIONAL VERSION   5
    MARK 8:17-19 NEW INTERNATIONAL VERSION   6
    2 TIMOTHY 4:2-4 KING JAMES VERSION   6
    REVELATION 2:10-12 NEW INTERNATIONAL VERSION   6
    2 PETER 1:20-21 EASY-TO-READ VERSION   6
    1 SAMUEL 2:26-35 EASY-TO-READ VERSION   7
    SUMMARY   8
    EPHESIANS 1:2 KING JAMES VERSION   9
DEVINE INSIGHTS FROM ABOVE   11
    EPHESIANS 1:3 KING JAMES VERSION   11
    EPHESIANS 1:4-6 KING JAMES VERSION   11
    EPHESIANS 1:4-6 EASY-TO-READ VERSION   12
    ECCLESIASTES 7:20 AMPLIFIED BIBLE   13
    ROMANS 3:23-24 EASY-TO-READ VERSION   13
    ROMANS 2:11-15 AMPLIFIED BIBLE   13
    ROMANS 2:11-15 EASY-TO-READ VERSION   14
    ROMANS 2:14-16 EASY-TO-READ VERSION   15
    1 TIMOTHY 4:1-3 EASY-TO-READ VERSION   15

Titus 1:14-16 Easy-to-Read Version	15
1 Peter 3:20-22 Easy-to-Read Version	16
Summary	16
John 8:8-10 King James Version	16
Acts 24:15-17 King James Version	17
Romans 2:14-16 King James Version	17
Romans 2:14-16 Easy-to-Read Version	17
Romans 9:1-3 King James Version	17
Romans 9:1-3 Easy-to-Read Version	18
1 Corinthians 8:11-13	18
King James Version	18
1 Corinthians 8:11-13 Easy-to-Read Version	18
2 Corinthians 1:11-13 Amplified Bible	18
Hebrews 9:13-15 King James Version	19
1 Peter 3:20-22 King James Version	19
1 Peter 3:20-22 Easy-to-Read Version	19
Romans 2:14-16 Amplified Bible	19
1 Samuel 2:34-36 King James Version	20
Exodus 35:20-22 King James Version	21
Jeremiah 32:37-40 King James Version	21
Ezekiel 11:15-20 King James Version	21
Matthew 13:18-25 Easy-to-Read Version	22
Jesus Explains the Story About Seed	22
Acts 2:45-47 King James Version	22
Acts 4:31-33 King James Version	23
Romans 2:14-16 King James Version	23
1 Corinthians 6:16-18 Easy-to-Read Version	23
Genesis 5:24 Easy-to-Read Version	23
Ephesians 4:1-15 King James Version	24
Philippians 2:1-3 Easy-to-Read Version	24
Romans 15:4-6 King James Version	25
Romans 15:4-12 Amplified Bible	25

COMPARE THE PROPHETIC UTTERANCE IN REVELATION AND THE BOOK OF EPHESIANS   27

Revelation 2:1-7 King James Version (KJV)	27
Acts 11:1-18 King James Version (KJV)	28
Ephesians 2:5-9 Easy-to-Read Version	30
Ephesians 4:17-32 Amplified Bible (AMP)	31
Summary	34
2 Timothy 4:2-4 King James Version (KJV)	36

GRACE AND WHAT IT MEANS.   39

Ephesians 1:4-16 King James Version	39

GALATIANS 3:26-29 KING JAMES VERSION	40
GALATIANS 3:26-29 EASY-TO-READ VERSION	40
EPHESIANS 2:4-6 KING JAMES VERSION	40
JOHN 1:15-17 KING JAMES VERSION	41
ACTS 15:5-12 EASY-TO-READ VERSION	41
ACTS 20:31-32 EASY-TO-READ VERSION	42
JOHN 8:41-43 EASY-TO-READ VERSION	42
JOHN 14:14-16 EASY-TO-READ VERSION	42
JOHN 14:22-30 EASY-TO-READ VERSION	43
REVELATION 2 EASY-TO-READ VERSION	43
JOHN 14:22-30 EASY-TO-READ VERSION	44
2 PETER 3:8-10 EASY-TO-READ VERSION	45
ACTS 9:1-25 EASY-TO-READ VERSION	46
ACTS 9:21 WHO TRUST IN JESUS LITERALLY, "WHO CALL ON THIS NAME."	48
REVELATION 2:19-21 KING JAMES VERSION	48
SUMMARY	48
ROMANS 3:26-28 AMPLIFIED BIBLE	49
EPHESIANS 2:8-10 EASY-TO-READ VERSION	49
PSALM 51:1-12 KING JAMES VERSION	50
REVELATION 2:1-7 EASY-TO-READ VERSION	51
JOHN 9:1-38 KING JAMES VERSION (KJV)	52
EPHESIANS 2:4-8 EASY-TO-READ VERSION	54
GOOD WORKS, HOW THEY BECOME A DRIVING FORCE IN US	**55**
EPHESIANS 2:1-8 EASY-TO-READ VERSION	55
1 JOHN 3:18 KING JAMES VERSION	56
1 JOHN 3:18 EASY-TO-READ VERSION	56
ISAIAH 5:19-21 KING JAMES VERSION	57
EPHESIANS 6:11-13 AMPLIFIED BIBLE	57
EPHESIANS 6:11-13 EASY-TO-READ VERSION	57
PSALM 14:1-3 AMPLIFIED BIBLE	58
2 CHRONICLES 7:10-15 KING JAMES VERSION	59
JOB 31:3-10 NEW INTERNATIONAL VERSION	59
ISAIAH 55:7-9 KING JAMES VERSION	60
EPHESIANS 2:1-3 KING JAMES VERSION	60
EPHESIANS 4:11-25 EASY-TO-READ VERSION	61
ZECHARIAH 8:16 EASY-TO-READ VERSION	62
EPHESIANS 5:1-20 KING JAMES VERSION	62
SUMMARY	63
1 JOHN 3:18 KING JAMES VERSION	63
1 JOHN 3:18 EASY-TO-READ VERSION	63
LUKE 10:25-37 EASY-TO-READ VERSION	70

DEUTERONOMY 6:5 EASY-TO-READ VERSION	71
LEVITICUS 19:18 EASY-TO-READ VERSION	71
THE BASIS OF OUR SIN; OUR SELFISH NATURE	**73**
EPHESIANS 2:1-8 EASY-TO-READ VERSION	73
REVELATION 2:18-29 KING JAMES VERSION (KJV)	74
PROVERBS 16:24-26 AMPLIFIED BIBLE	75
EXODUS 20:17 AMPLIFIED BIBLE	76
PSALM 81:11-13 KING JAMES VERSION	76
1 JOHN 2:15-17 KING JAMES VERSION	76
1 JOHN 2:15-17 AMPLIFIED BIBLE	76
1 CORINTHIANS 13:2-13 KING JAMES VERSION (KJV)	78
EPHESIANS 4:1-10 KING JAMES VERSION	79
GALATIANS 3:27-29 KING JAMES VERSION	79
COLOSSIANS 3:10-12 KING JAMES VERSION	79
ROMANS 12:1-3 KING JAMES VERSION (KJV)	80
TITUS 2:11-15 KING JAMES VERSION (KJV)	80
ACTS 8:1-25 KING JAMES VERSION (KJV)	81
EPHESIANS 3:10-12 AMPLIFIED BIBLE	83
EXODUS 7:9-12 KING JAMES VERSION (KJV)	83
ACTS 13:5-7 KING JAMES VERSION (KJV)	84
SUMMARY	84
MATTHEW 18:6-8 AMPLIFIED BIBLE	85
MARK 4:18-20 AMPLIFIED BIBLE	85
JOHN 12:45-47 AMPLIFIED BIBLE	85
EPHESIANS 5:1-10 EASY-TO-READ VERSION	86
ISAIAH 57:11-13 EASY-TO-READ VERSION	86
EPHESIANS 2:1-8 EASY-TO-READ VERSION 88	
EPHESIANS 4:17-32 AMPLIFIED BIBLE	89
EPHESIANS 5:1-20 AMPLIFIED BIBLE	90
PAUL EXPLAINS OUR DEFENSIVE TOOLS TO RESIST SINFUL INFLUENCES	**93**
EPHESIANS 3 KING JAMES VERSION	93
EPHESIANS 5:1-20 AMPLIFIED BIBLE	94
EPHESIANS 6:10-18 AMPLIFIED BIBLE	96
PROVERBS 23:6-8 KING JAMES VERSION	98
PROVERBS 23:6-8 AMPLIFIED BIBLE	98
JAMES 1:14-15 KING JAMES VERSION	99
JAMES 1:14-15 AMPLIFIED BIBLE	99
LUKE 21:33-35 AMPLIFIED BIBLE	99
SECTION 76:4A-4F DOCTRINE & COVENANTS	99
MATTHEW 15:16-18 AMPLIFIED BIBLE	100

Mark 7:21-23 King James Version	100
Ephesians 6:10-18 King James Version	101
Ephesians 2:7-9 King James Version	103
Hebrews 4:11-13 King James Version	104
Hebrews 4:11-13 Amplified Bible	104
Matthew 15:11-20 Amplified Bible	105
1 Thessalonians 4:1-3 Amplified Bible	106
Ephesians 4:29-31 Amplified Bible	106
1 Corinthians 13 King James Version	107
Ephesians 4:31-32 Amplified Bible	107
Ephesians 5:18-20 King James Version	108
Ephesians 5:18-20 Easy-to-Read Version	108
Summary	108
Deuteronomy 32:42-44 King James Version	109
Romans 12:18-20 King James Version	109
Isaiah 59:10-18 Amplified Bible	109
Matthew 5:21-23 Amplified Bible	111
1 Corinthians 13:1-8 King James Version	112
Luke 6:34-36 King James Version	112
Ephesians 5:18-20 King James Version	112
Ephesians 5:18-20 Easy-to-Read Version	113
Matthew 6:30-34 Amplified Bible	113
1 Peter 1:21-23 King James Version	114
Ezekiel 11:18-20 King James Version	114
Ezekiel 36:25-27 King James Version	115
Romans 7:5-7 Easy-to-Read Version	115
John 5:28-30 Easy-to-Read Version	115
Proverbs 12:1-3 Easy-to-Read Version	116
Jude 1-10 Easy-to-Read Version	116
Micah 7:1-3 Easy-to-Read Version	117
Colossians 3 Inspired Version	118
Colossians 4 Inspired Version	119
Revelation 3:7-13 King James Version (KJV)	119
Isaiah 61:10 King James Version	120
Ephesians 6:10-18 King James Version	120
God Has to Have a Holy and Righteous People to Dwell With Him	**123**
Psalm 51:6-12 Amplified Bible	123
1 Timothy 1:4-6 King James Version	123
1 Timothy 1:4-6 Amplified Bible	124
1 Peter 1:21-23 King James Version	124
Colossians 3 Inspired Version	124

Colossians 4 Inspired Version	126
Ephesians 1:3-11 King James Version	126
Ephesians 4:11-32 King James Version	126
Job 34:11 Easy-to-Read Version	128
Romans 2:1-6 Easy-to-Read Version	128
1 Corinthians 15:35-42 King James Version	129
Revelation 2:19-21 Easy-to-Read Version	129
Exodus 19:5-7 Amplified Bible	130
Ephesians 1:3-5 King James Version	130
Ephesians 2:20-22 Amplified Bible	131
Ephesians 5:26-27 King James Version	131
Summary	132
Revelation 2:8-11 Amplified Bible	132
Matthew 25:20-22 King James Version (KJV)	133
John 14:21 Easy-to-Read Version	134
JESUS WHO HE IS AND HIS LOVE AND HIS PURPOSE	**143**
Ephesians 1:1-14 King James Version	143
Ephesians 5:1-2 King James Version	144
Ephesians 6:5-6 King James Version	144
Summary	155
WHAT LIES BEFORE US?	**159**
Ephesians 4:23-25 Easy-to-Read Version	159
Zechariah 8:16 Easy-to-Read Version	159
Genesis 8:20-22 Amplified Bible	159
Ephesians 2:15-17 King James Version	160
Ephesians 2:15-17 Amplified Bible	160
Ephesians 3:5-7 King James Version	160
Ephesians 4:3-7 King James Version	160
Ephesians 4:3-7 Amplified Bible	161
Ephesians 4:22-26 King James Version	161
Ephesians 4:22-26 Amplified Bible	161
Ephesians 5:28-32 King James Version	162
Ephesians 5:28-32 Amplified Bible	162
Galatians 3:27-29 King James Version	163
Luke 22:19-29 Easy-to-Read Version	163
Ephesians 2:1-10 King James Version	165
Psalm 24:3-5 King James Version	165
Romans 2:28-29 King James Version	165
Mark 7:21-23 King James Version	166
Ephesians 2:8-10 King James Version	166
Romans 7:3-5 Easy-to-Read Version	167
Romans 12:4-6 Easy-to-Read Version	167

MATTHEW 5:44-46 KING JAMES VERSION	167
LUKE 13:1-3 EASY-TO-READ VERSION	168
1 CORINTHIANS 12:25-27 EASY-TO-READ VERSION	168
JEREMIAH 1:5-10 EASY-TO-READ VERSION	169
JEREMIAH 24:5-7 EASY-TO-READ VERSION	169
JUDE 19-21 EASY-TO-READ VERSION	170
1 THESSALONIANS 5:10-12 AMPLIFIED BIBLE	170
LUKE 12:35-37 EASY-TO-READ VERSION	170
ROMANS 6:4-8 EASY-TO-READ VERSION	171
2 CORINTHIANS 13:3-8 EASY-TO-READ VERSION	171
PHILIPPIANS 3:18-21 EASY-TO-READ VERSION	171
EASY-TO-READ VERSION WE ARE GOD'S CHILDREN	172
SUMMARY	172
EPHESIANS 2:15-17 KING JAMES VERSION	173
EPHESIANS 2:15-17 AMPLIFIED BIBLE	173
COLOSSIANS 1:13-14 KING JAMES VERSION	173
HEBREWS 11:30-40 KING JAMES VERSION	174
1 PETER 2:9-13 AMPLIFIED BIBLE	174
1 JOHN 3:1-10 KING JAMES VERSION	175
1 JOHN 5:11-12 REVISED STANDARD VERSION	176
POSTSCRIPT	**177**
APPENDIX	**179**
INDEX	**181**
SCRIPTURE REFERENCES	**189**
ABOUT THE AUTHOR	**197**

About the Author

OR SCRIBE (AS I SEE IT)

Lorenzo Hill and his wife Clotilde right after marriage, 1969

Lorenzo Hill and his wife Clotilde after 49 years, 2018
We have now been married 52 years As of April 2020

Lorenzo Hill has served in the ministry of the Community of Christ (formerly The Reorganized Church of Jesus Christ Of Latter Day Saints) since 1976, when he was ordained a priest. Throughout his ministry, he has been a self-supporting minister. He has served in his current office of Evangelist since 1988 and continues to be active in ministry, serving in various roles of leadership and other roles in which he is called to serve. His passion has been providing guidance to youth. He had to sadly stop this part of his ministry for health reasons. He provides ongoing ministry through his commitment to spreading word in preaching and bringing ministry to the sick in soul and body.

Lorenzo was raised in St. Louis Missouri and resided there until he received his Bachelor of Science degree in Chemical Engineering in 1970 from the University of Missouri at Rolla (currently known as the Missouri School of Science and Technology). He is a registered retired professional engineer. He has worked in the petroleum industry since he graduated from college and has retired twice. He has moved around quite a bit. He has been blessed to be able to see many other countries because of his employment and for pleasure. The Holy Spirit has used this to open his eyes to the suffering that many experiences in this life due to governmental policies and personal lifestyles.

He has been married to his wife, Clotilde, for 54 years. She has been his constant support in all his endeavors. They have three children: two daughters Alicia Renee Hill, Reynada Charlese Robinson, and one son, Jared Lorenzo Hill.

Although he has taken many post-graduate courses in both engineering and ministry, Lorenzo chose not to pursue an advanced degree. He has authored numerous technical reports and technical texts for the training and instruction of engineers and construction inspectors. All these works, however, were prepared for either clients or for internal company use and as such, were not issued as external publications.

He has been inspired to publish five other books. These books are titled:

Formulas in The Scripture: $E = MC^2$
And
What God Intends for Us in His Commandments

**And
Eternal Life
And
What God is Saying in the Book of Revelation: Part 1
And
What God is Saying in the Book of Revelation: Part 2**

These works are currently in print and can be purchased on Amazon.com in paperback or e-book format. They may also be found on Apple books in e-book format.

If there is one way to express His walk with Christ, there are some words from a hymn in our Church entitled Admonition. These are as follows:

"Grace waits upon the souls who try."

As Paul states I am not perfect yet, but I strive for the high calling of Christ Jesus and await the transformation to be like Him in all ways.
Thanks to my wife and daughters for proofreading these works. Praise be to God for His inspiring spirit, enlightenment, and encouragement. It is by God's grace I have been allowed to present His intent and purposes in these books so that we may all know the truth of the Gospel.